P9-DEC-598

# Chapter 1: Introduction To Financial Reporting

Chapter 1 - Problem 1 - Supply the Words Necessary to Complete
                the Following Items

1. The users of the financial statements use the financial
   statements to make _____.

2. The _____ for financial reports is derived from the
   perceived improvement in _____ - _____.

3. Generally accepted accounting principles (GAAP) are
   accounting principles that have _____

   _____ _____.

4. The Securities Act of 1933 was intended to regulate the
   _____ offering and sale of securities in _____

   _____.

5. In general, the Securities Act of 1934 was intended to
   regulate securities trading on the _____ _____,
   and it was under this authority that the _____ and
   _____ _____ was created.

6. The _____ is a professional accounting organization
   whose members are certified public accountants (CPAs).

7. In 1972, a special study group of the AICPA recommended
   another approach - the establishment of the _____

   _____ _____ _____.

8. The FASAC is responsible for advising the _____.

9. The FASB issues four types of pronouncements: _____
   of _____ _____ _____ , Interpretations,
   Technical bulletins, and _____ of _____

   _____ _____ .

10. The FASB standard-setting process includes aspects of
    accounting _____ and _____ _____.

11. The FASB Conceptual Framework is intended to set forth a
    system of interrelated _____ and underlying _____ that
    will serve as the basis for evaluating existing standards of
    financial accounting and reporting.

12. _____ and _____ are the two primary qualities that make accounting information useful for _____ making.

13. These characteristics of accounting information that make it a desirable commodity can be viewed as a hierarchy of qualities, with _____ and _____ for decision making of most importance.

14. SFAC No. 5 identifies _____ different _____ attributes currently used in practice.

15. The EITF has become a very important source of _____. They have the capability to review a number of issues within a relatively short period of time. This greatly contrasts with the deliberations that go into a(n) _____.

16. In all cases, the reports are to be a "fair _____." Even when there is an explicit GAAP, following the GAAP is not appropriate unless the end result is a "_____ _____."

17. If, in reality, a particular entity is threatened with bankruptcy or liquidation, then the _____ - _____ assumption should be dropped.

18. With the _____ _____ assumption, inaccuracies of accounting for the entity short of its complete life span are accepted.

19. Some businesses select an accounting period that ends when operations are at a low ebb. This type of period is known as a _____ _____ year. Some businesses select a twelve-month accounting period closing at the end of a month other than December; this is known as a _____ _____.

20. The loss in value of money is called _____.

21. Using the concept of _____ the measurement with the least favorable effect on _____ _____ and financial position in the _____ _____ is selected.

22. With the _____ _____, the basic intent is to determine the revenue first and then _____ the appropriate cost against this revenue.

PAYNE

# Financial Reporting & Analysis:
## Using Financial Accounting Information

### 8th Edition

## Charles H. Gibson

The University of Toledo

SOUTH-WESTERN
★
THOMSON LEARNING

Australia · Canada · Mexico · Singapore · Spain · United Kingdom · United States

Financial Reporting Analysis:  Using Financial Accounting Information Study Guide, 8e
    by Gibson

Acquisitions Editor:  Rochelle Kronzek
Senior Developmental Editor:  Ken Martin
Marketing Manager:  Larry Qualls
Production Editor:  Marci Dechter
Manufacturing Coordinator:  Doug Wilke
Cover Design:  Modern Design
Cover Image:  copyright 1999 PhotoDisc
Printer:  Globus

COPYRIGHT ©2001 by South-Western College Publishing, a division of Thomson Learning.
The Thomson Learning logo is a registered trademark used herein under license.

**All Rights Reserved.** No part of this work covered by the copyright hereon may be reproduced or
used in any form or by any means – graphic, electronic, or mechanical, including photocopying,
recording, taping, or information storage and retrieval systems – without the written permission of
the publisher.

Printed in the United States of America
1  2  3  4  5  03  02  01  00

For more information contact South-Western College Publishing, 5101 Madison Road,
Cincinnati, Ohio, 45227 or find us on the Internet at http://www.swcollege.com
**For permission to use material from this text or product,contact us by**
• **telephone:  1-800-730-2214**
• **fax:  1-800-730-2215**
• **web:  http://www.thomsonrights.com**


ISBN:  0-324-02356-1

This book is printed on acid-free paper.

**PREFACE**

This Study Guide is designed to help you make an effective use of your study time and help you master the material in Financial Reporting and Analysis:  Using Financial Accounting Information.  Problems are included to assist you with the review of chapter material.  The following types of problems are provided:

1.  Supply the Words Necessary to Complete the Following Items

2.  Multiple Choice

3.  True/False

4.  Matching

5.  Selected Problems

GOOD LUCK!

# TABLE OF CONTENTS

23. The _____ concept requires the entity to give the same treatment to comparable transactions from _____ to _____.

24. The _____ concept involves the relative size and importance of an item to a firm.

25. Many important events that influence the prospects for the entity are not recorded, and, therefore, they are not reflected in the _____ _____ because they fall outside the _____ _____.

26. The cash basis recognizes revenue when cash is _____ and recognizes expenses when cash is _____.

27. The use of the accrual basis complicates the accounting process, but the end result is considered more _____ than the _____ basis.


## Chapter 1 - Problem 2 - Multiple Choice

Choose the best answer for each of the following questions and enter the identifying letter in the space provided.

_____ 1. The organization that has by federal law the primary responsibility and authority for the development of financial accounting.

   a. New York Stock Exchange
   b. Securities and Exchange Commission
   c. Accounting Principles Board
   d. Financial Accounting Standards Board
   e. AICPA Committee on Accounting Procedure

_____ 2. The organization in the private sector that currently has the primary leadership responsibility for the development of financial accounting.

   a. Securities and Exchange Commission
   b. American Institute of Certified Public Accountants
   c. Financial Accounting Standards Board
   d. Accounting Principles Board
   e. New York Stock Exchange

_____ 3. Recording revenue at the point of sale would be an example of the application of:

   a. conservatism.
   b. matching.
   c. realization.
   d. going concern.
   e. objectivity.

_____ 4. Charging off equipment that cost an immaterial amount in the period acquired would be an example of the application of:

   a. materiality.
   b. matching.
   c. time period.
   d. historical cost.
   e. going concern principle.

_____ 5. The assumption that allows accountants to accept some inaccuracy, because of incomplete information about the future, in exchange for more timely reporting.

   a. conservatism
   b. time period
   c. business entity
   d. materiality
   e. realization

_____ 6. Overstating expenses is justified based on:

   a. time period assumption.
   b. conservatism assumption.
   c. materiality assumption.
   d. matching assumption.
   e. none of the above.

_____ 7. Valuing assets at their liquidation values is consistent with:

   a. time period assumption.
   b. going concern assumption.
   c. matching assumption.
   d. conservatism assumption.
   e. none of the above.

4

_____ 8. At the end of the fiscal year, an adjusting entry is made which increases insurance expense and decreases prepaid insurance. This entry is an application of which accounting principle?

    a. full disclosure
    b. materiality
    c. matching
    d. objectivity
    e. realization

_____ 9. Accountants provide for inflation using the following accounting principle:

    a. monetary unit.
    b. historical cost.
    c. realization.
    d. going concern.
    e. none of the above.

_____ 10. Which assumption of the accounting model involves the relative size and importance of an item to a firm?

    a. going concern
    b. time period
    c. conservatism
    d. materiality
    e. realization

_____ 11. The entity should give the same treatment to comparable transactions from period to period. This represents the application of which principle?

    a. full disclosure
    b. objectivity
    c. materiality
    d. consistency
    e. time period assumption

_____ 12. The accountant only records events that affect the financial position of the entity and, at the same time, can be reasonably determined in monetary terms. This describes which of the following terms:

    a. materiality
    b. industry practice
    c. transaction approach
    d. full disclosure
    e. consistency

_____ 13. An accounting period that ends at December 31:

    a. a calendar year
    b. a fiscal year
    c. natural business year
    d. an operating year
    e. none of the above

_____ 14. The accounting principle that assumes that the firm will stay in business for an indefinite period of time.

    a. monetary unit
    b. historical cost
    c. realization
    d. going concern
    e. none of the above

_____ 15. The realization principle addresses when to recognize revenue. The related principle that addresses when to recognize the cost.

    a. matching
    b. going concern
    c. consistency
    d. materiality
    e. none of the above

_____ 16. Which of these measurement attributes is currently used in practice?

    a. historical cost
    b. current cost
    c. current market value
    d. present value
    e. all of the above are used in practice

_____ 17. Which of these is not currently used in practice to recognize revenue?

    a. receipt of order
    b. point of sale
    c. end of production
    d. during production
    e. receipt of cash

Chapter 1 - Problem 3 - True/False

Indicate whether each of the following is true (T) or false (F) in the space provided.

_____ 1. Some industry practices lead to accounting reports that do not conform to the general theory that underlies accounting.

_____ 2. The objectivity concept requires the accountant to only use objective verifiable data.

_____ 3. Immaterial items are not subject to the concepts and principles that bind the accountant.

_____ 4. Financial statements that are prepared using the going concern concept are misleading if the firm does not continue as a going concern.

_____ 5. Using generally accepted accounting principles, the decision is made to accept some inaccuracy, because of incomplete information about the future, in exchange for more timely reporting.

_____ 6. In order to determine the economic success of a business, we should view it as separate from the other resources of the owners.

_____ 7. Accountants normally recognize revenue when the production process is completed.

_____ 8. The historical cost of an item and the item's fair market value are usually the same.

_____ 9. The statements of Financial Accounting Concepts are intended to provide the Financial Accounting Standards Board with a common foundation and the basic underlying reasoning on which to consider the merits of various alternative accounting principles.

_____ 10. Generally accepted accounting principles assume that the reader of the financial statements is primarily interested in the liquidation values.

_____ 11. The going concern assumption influences the classification of assets and liabilities.

_____ 12. Money is an acceptable vehicle for measuring financial transactions.

_____ 13. A gain in value of money is called inflation.

_____ 14. Accountants normally recognize revenue at the point of sale.

_____ 15. The Statements of Financial Accounting Standards are intended to provide the Financial Accounting Standards Board with a common foundation and the basic underlying reasoning on which to consider the merits of various alternative accounting principles.

_____ 16. The Financial Accounting Standards Board considers the Financial Accounting Concepts when considering new standards.

_____ 17. Financial Accounting Concepts (FACs) do not establish generally accepted accounting principles.

_____ 18. The time period assumption indicates that the entity will remain in business for a definite period of time.

_____ 19. Accounting information should be understandable to all users.

_____ 20. To be reliable, accounting information should have either predictive or feedback value, or both. In addition, it should be timely.

_____ 21. Decision usefulness is the overall qualitative characteristic to be used in judging the quality of accounting information.

_____ 22. Reasonable inaccuracies of accounting for an entity short of its complete life span are not accepted.

# Chapter 1 - Problem 4 - Matching Concepts: Accounting Assumptions and Conventions

Listed below are several accounting principles and assumptions. Match the letter that goes with each statement.

a. business entity     g. realization
b. going concern     h. consistency
c. time period     i. full disclosure
d. monetary unit     j. objectivity
e. historical cost     k. materiality
f. conservatism     l. matching

_____ 1. Requires the accountant to adhere as closely as possible to verifiable data.

_____ 2. Involves the relative size and importance of an item to a firm.

_____ 3. Assumptions that the business for which the financial statements are prepared is separate and distinct from the owners of the entity.

_____ 4. The assumption that the entity that is being accounted for will remain in business for an indefinite period of time.

_____ 5. The same treatment is given to comparable transactions from period to period.

_____ 6. Directs that the measurement that has the least favorable effect on net income and financial position in the current period be selected.

_____ 7. The appropriate cost to be charged against the revenue.

# Chapter 1 - Problem 5 - Matching Concepts - Qualitative Characteristics

Listed below are several qualitative characteristics.  Match the letter (or letters) that goes with each statement.

a.  understandability
b.  usefulness for decision making
c.  relevance
d.  reliability
e.  predictive
f.  feedback value
g.  timely

h.  verifiable
i.  representational
     faithfulness
j.  neutrality
k.  comparability
l.  materiality
m.  benefits of information
     should exceed its cost


_____  1.  Interacts with relevance and reliability to contribute to the usefulness of information.

_____  2.  Two constraints included in the hierarchy.

_____  3.  Two primary qualities that make accounting information useful for decision making.

_____  4.  For this quality the information needs to have predictive and feedback value and be timely.

_____  5.  For this quality the information must be verifiable, subject to represential faithfulness, and neutral.

_____  6.  These are the qualitative characteristics that are viewed as having the most importance.

_____  7.  SFAC No. 2 indicates that, to be relevant, the information needs to have these characteristics.

_____  8.  SFAC No. 2 indicates that, to be reliable, the information needs to have these characteristics.

Chapter 1 - Problem 6 - Matching Concepts
"Elements of Financial Statements"

Listed below are the ten "Elements of Financial Statements" per SFAC No. 6. Match the letter that goes with each definition.

a. assets
b. equity
c. losses
d. gains
e. investment by owners

f. comprehensive income
g. distribution to owners
h. revenues
i. liabilities
j. expenses

_____ 1. Probable future economic benefits obtained or controlled by a particular entity as a result of past transactions or events.

_____ 2. Residual interest in the assets of an entity that remains after deducting its liabilities.

_____ 3. A decrease in equity of a particular business enterprise resulting from transferring assets, rendering services, or incurring liabilities by the enterprise to owners.

_____ 4. Inflows or other enhancements of assets of an entity or settlements of its liabilities (or a combination of both) from delivering or producing goods, rendering services, or other activities that constitute the entity's ongoing major or central operations.

_____ 5. Increases in equity (net assets) from peripheral or incidental transactions of an entity and from all other transactions and other events) and circumstances affecting the entity during a period except those that result from revenues or investments by owners.

_____ 6. Probable future sacrifices of economic benefits arising from present obligations of a particular entity to transfer assets or provide services to other entities in the future as a result of past transactions or events.

_____ 7. Increases in equity of a particular business enterprise resulting from transfers to the enterprise from other entities of something of value to obtain or increase ownership interests (or equity) in it.

_____ 8. The change in equity (net assets) of a business enterprise during a period from transactions and other events and circumstances from nonowner sources. It includes all changes in equity during a period except those resulting from investments by owners and distributions to owners.

_____ 9. Outflows or other consumption or using up of assets or incurrences of liabilities (or a combination of both) from delivering or producing goods, rendering services, or carrying out other activities that constitute the entity's ongoing major or central operations.

_____ 10. Decreases in equity (net assets) from peripheral or incidental transactions of an entity and from all other transactions and other events and circumstances affecting the entity during a period except those that result from expenses or distributions to owners.

Chapter 1 - Problem 7 - Matching Acronyms

Listed below are phrases with the appropriate acronym. Match the letter that goes with each definition.

a.  generally accepted accounting principles (GAAP)
b.  securities and exchange commission (SEC)
c.  financial reporting releases (FRRs)
d.  American institute of certified public accountants (AICPA)
e.  certified public accountants (CPAs)
f.  accounting principles board (APB)
g.  accounting principles board opinions (APBO)
h.  accounting principles board statements (APBS)
i.  financial accounting standards board (FASB)
j.  financial accounting foundation (FAF)
k.  financial accounting standards advisory council (FASAC)
l.  statements of financial standards (SFAS)
m.  statements of financial accounting concepts (SFAC)
n.  discussion memorandum (DM)
o.  exposure draft (ED)
p.  accounting standards executive committee (ASEC)
q.  statements of position (SOP)
r.  emerging issues task force (EITF)

_____ 1. Accounting principles that have substantial authoritative support.

_____ 2. A task force of representatives from the accounting profession created by the FASB to deal with emerging issues of financial reporting.

_____ 3. A proposed statement of financial accounting standards (SFAS).

_____ 4. Issued by the Accounting Standards Division of the AICPA to influence the development of accounting standards.

_____ 5. Created by the Securities Exchange Act of 1934.

_____ 6. A professional accounting organization whose members are certified public accountants (CPAs).

_____ 7. Issued official opinions on accounting standards between 1959-1973.

_____ 8. Represent views of the Accounting Principles Board but not the official opinions.

_____ 9. This board issues four types of pronouncements: (1) Statements of Financial Accounting Standards (CSFAS), (2) Interpretations, (3) Technical bulletins, and (4) Statements of Financial Accounting Concepts (SFAC).

_____ 10. Governs the Financial Accounting Standards Board (FASB).

_____ 11. These statements are issued by the Financial Accounting Standards Board (FASB), and establish GAAP for specific accounting issues.

_____ 12. These Statements are issued by the Financial Accounting Standards Board (FASB), and provide a theoretical foundation upon which to base GAAP. They are not part of GAAP.

_____ 13. Serves as the official voice of the AICPA in matters relating to financial accounting and reporting standards.

_____ 14. Presents all known facts and points of view on a topic. Issued by the FASB.

_____ 15. Responsible for advising the FASB.

_____ 16. Represented official positions of the APB.

_____ 17. An accountant who has received a certificate stating that he/she has met the requirements of state law.

_____ 18. Issued by the SEC and give the SEC's official position on matters relating to financial statements.

## Chapter 1 - Problem 8 - Matching Concept Statements

Listed below are Concept Statements. Match the letter that goes with each Concept Statement title.

a. Statement of Financial Accounting Concepts No. 1.
b. Statement of Financial Accounting Concepts No. 2.
c. Statement of Financial Accounting Concepts No. 3.
d. Statement of Financial Accounting Concepts No. 4.
e. Statement of Financial Accounting Concepts No. 5.
f. Statement of Financial Accounting Concepts No. 6.
g. Statement of Financial Accounting Concepts No. 7.

_____ 1.   Elements of Financial Statements (a replacement of No. 3).

_____ 2.   Objectives of Financial Reporting by Nonbusiness Organizations.

_____ 3.   Objectives of Financial Reporting by Business Enterprises.

_____ 4.   Elements of Financial Statements of Business Enterprises.

_____ 5.   Recognition and Measurement in Financial Statements of Business Enterprises.

_____ 6.   Qualitative Characteristics of Accounting Information.

_____ 7.   Using Cash Flow Information in Accounting Measurements.

# Chapter 1 - Problem 9 - Determine Income on an Accrual Basis and on a Cash Basis

These data relate to Zink Company for the year ended December 31, 2001:

| | |
|---|---:|
| Sales on credit | $100,000 |
| Cost of inventory sold on credit | 70,000 |
| Collections from customers | 50,000 |
| Purchase of inventory on credit | 60,000 |
| Payment for purchases | 65,000 |
| Selling expenses (accrual basis) | 15,000 |
| Payment for selling expenses | 20,000 |

Required:  1.  Determine income on an accrual basis.
            2.  Determine income on a cash basis.

Chapter 1 - Problem 10 - Determine Income on an Accrual Basis and
            on a Cash Basis

These data relate to Gem Company for the year ended December 31,
2001:

| | |
|---|---:|
| Sales on credit | $250,000 |
| Cost of inventory sold on credit | 150,000 |
| Collections from customers | 230,000 |
| Purchase of inventory on credit | 220,000 |
| Payment of purchases | 180,000 |
| Selling expenses (accrual basis) | 50,000 |
| Payment of selling expenses | 40,000 |

Required:   1.   Determine income on an accrual basis.
            2.   Determine income on a cash basis.

# CHAPTER 1 - SOLUTIONS

## Chapter 1- Problem 1 - Supply the Words Necessary to Complete the Following Items

1. decisions

2. demand; decision-making

3. substantial authoritative support

4. initial; interstate commerce

5. national exchanges; Securities and Exchange Commission

6. AICPA

7. Financial Accounting Standards Board

8. FASB

9. Statement of Financial Accounting Standards; Statements of Financial Accounting Concepts

10. theory; political concepts

11. objectives; concepts

12. Relevance; reliability; decision

13. understandability; usefulness

14. five; measurement

15. GAAP; SFAS

16. representation; fair representation

17. going-concern

18. time period

19. natural business; fiscal year

20. inflation

21. conservatism; net income; current period

22. matching concept; match

23. consistency; period to period

24. materiality

25. financial statements; transaction approach

26. received; paid

27. representative; cash

## Chapter 1 - Problem 2 - Multiple Choice

___b___ 1. In effect, the SEC has the authority to determine GAAP and to regulate the accounting profession.

___c___ 2. The Financial Accounting Standards Board currently has the primary leadership responsibility for the development of financial accounting.

___c___ 3. The realization principle deals with when to recognize revenue. Recording revenue at the point of sale is an example of the application of the realization principle.

___a___ 4. Immaterial items are not subject to the concepts and principles that bind the accountant.

___b___ 5. With the time period assumption, we accept some inaccuracies of accounting for the entity short of its complete life span. We assume that the entity can be accounted for with reasonable accuracy for a particular period of time.

___e___ 6. Accountants do not have an assumption that justifies overstating expenses.

___e___ 7. The going-concern assumption deliberately disregards the possibility that the entity will go bankrupt or be liquidated. Therefore, valuing assets at their liquidation values is <u>not</u> consistent with the going concern assumption.

___c___ 8. The matching concept addresses when to recognize the costs associated with the recognized revenue.

___e___ 9. None of the traditional assumptions provide for inflation.

___d___ 10. The concept that exempts immaterial items from GAAP.

___d___ 11. The consistency concept requires the entity to give the same treatment to comparable transactions from period to period.

<u>  c  </u>  12.  Many important events that influence the prospects for the entity are not recorded and, therefore, are not reflected in the financial statements because they fall outside the transaction approach.

<u>  a  </u>  13.  The calendar year ends the accounting period on December 31.

<u>  d  </u>  14.  The going-concern assumption, that the entity in question will remain in business for an indefinite period of time, provides perspective on the future of the entity.

<u>  a  </u>  15.  The revenue realization concept involves when to recognize revenue. Accountants need a related concept that addresses when to recognize the costs associated with the recognized revenue: the matching concept.

<u>  e  </u>  16.  Historical cost, current cost, current market value, and present value are all used in practice.

<u>  a  </u>  17.  Receipt of order is not currently used in practice to recognize revenue.

## Chapter 1- Problem 3 - True/False

| | | | | | |
|---|---|---|---|---|---|
| T | 1. | T | 9. | T | 17. |
| F | 2. | F | 10. | F | 18. |
| T | 3. | T | 11. | F | 19. |
| T | 4. | T | 12. | F | 20. |
| T | 5. | F | 13. | T | 21. |
| T | 6. | T | 14. | F | 22. |
| F | 7. | F | 15. | | |
| F | 8. | T | 16. | | |

## Chapter 1 - Problem 4 - Matching Concepts - Accounting Assumptions and Conventions

| | | | |
|---|---|---|---|
| j | 1. | h | 5. |
| k | 2. | f | 6. |
| a | 3. | l | 7. |
| b | 4. | | |

## Chapter 1 - Problem 5 - Matching Concepts - Qualitative Characteristics

| | | | | | |
|---|---|---|---|---|---|
| k | 1. | c | 4. | e,f,g | 7. |
| l,m | 2. | d | 5. | h,i,j | 8. |
| c,d | 3. | a,b | 6. | | |

Chapter 1 - Problem 6 - Matching Concepts - "Elements of
                    Financial Statements"

| | | | |
|---|---|---|---|
| a | 1. | i | 6. |
| b | 2. | e | 7. |
| g | 3. | f | 8. |
| h | 4. | j | 9. |
| d | 5. | c | 10. |


Chapter 1 - Problem 7 - Matching Acronyms

| | | | | | |
|---|---|---|---|---|---|
| a | 1. | f | 7. | P | 13. |
| r | 2. | h | 8. | n | 14. |
| o | 3. | i | 9. | k | 15. |
| q | 4. | j | 10. | g | 16. |
| b | 5. | l | 11. | e | 17. |
| d | 6. | m | 12. | c | 18. |


Chapter 1 - Problem 8 - Matching Concept Statements

| | | | |
|---|---|---|---|
| f | 1. | e | 5. |
| d | 2. | b | 6. |
| a | 3. | g | 7. |
| c | 4. | | |


Chapter 1 - Problem 9 - Determine Income on an Accrual Basis and
                    on a Cash Basis

1.  Sales on credit                            $100,000
    Cost of inventory sold on credit            (70,000)
    Selling expenses                            (15,000)
    Income                                    $ 15,000

2.  Collections from customers                 $ 50,000
    Payment for purchases                       (65,000)
    Payment for selling expenses                (20,000)
    Loss                                      $(35,000)

# Chapter 1 - Problem 10 - Determine Income on an Accrual Basis and on a Cash Basis

1.  | | |
    |---|---:|
    | Sales on credit | $250,000 |
    | Cost of inventory sold on credit | (150,000) |
    | Selling expenses | (50,000) |
    | Income | $ 50,000 |

2.  | | |
    |---|---:|
    | Collections from customers | $230,000 |
    | Payment for purchases | (180,000) |
    | Payment for selling expenses | (40,000) |
    | Income | $ 10,000 |

# Chapter 2: Introduction to Financial Statements and Other Financial Reporting Topics

<u>Chapter 2 - Problem 1 - Supply the Words Necessary to Complete the Following Items</u>

1.  A business entity may be a sole proprietorship, a partnership, or a _____.

2.  Accounting for corporations, sole proprietorships, and partnerships is the same, except for the _____ _____.

3.  A balance sheet shows the financial condition of an accounting entity at a particular _____.

4.  Retained earnings _____ the balance sheet to the _____ _____.

5.  The income statement summarizes the result of operations for a particular _____ ___ _____.

6.  The statement of cash flows details the inflows and outflows of cash during a specified _____ __ _____.

7.  The statement of cash flows consists of three sections: cash flows from operating activities, cash flows from _____ _____, and cash flows from _____ _____.

8.  The _____ to the financial statements are used to present additional information about items included in the financial statements and to present additional _____ information.

9.  _____ _____ are dependent upon the occurrence or nonoccurrence of one or more future events to confirm the liability.

10. _____ _____ occur after the balance sheet date, but before the statements are issued.

11. A _____ is an event that causes a change in a company's assets, liabilities, or stockholders' equity, thus changing the company's _____ _____.

12. The _____ journals are designed to improve record keeping efficiency that could not be obtained by using only the _____ _____.

13. All _____ are recorded in a journal and are later posted from the journals to a _____ _____.

14. In a double-entry system, each _____ is recorded with the total dollar amount of the _____ equal to the total dollar amount of the _____.

15. With the double-entry system, debit merely means the _____ side of an account, while credit means the _____ side.

16. Asset, liability, and stockholders' equity accounts are referred to as _____ _____ because the balances in these accounts carry forward to the next accounting _____.

17. Balances in revenue, expense, gain, loss, and dividend accounts, described as _____ _____, are closed to _____ _____ and not carried into the next period.

18. Usually a company must use the _____ _____ to achieve a reasonable result for the balance sheet and the _____ _____.

19. Two of the principal financial statements, the _____ statement and the _____ _____, can be prepared directly from the adjusted accounts.

20. An _____ _____ is the formal statement of the auditor's opinion of the financial statements after conducting an _____.

21. From the point of view of analysis, financial statements accompanied by an _____ _____ without an explanatory paragraph or explanatory language carry the highest degree of _____.

22. A _____ consists principally of inquiries made to company personnel and analytical _____ applied to financial data.

23. The compilation report states that the accountant has not _____ or _____ the financial statements.

24. The _____ is responsible for conducting and independent examination of the statements and expressing an _____ on the financial statements based on the _____.

25. The SEC requires that a quarterly report (Form 10-Q), containing financial statements and a management discussion and analysis, be submitted within _____ days following the end of the _____.

26. The _____, which is the solicitation sent to stockholders for the election of directors and for the approval of other corporation actions, represents the stockholders' authorization regarding the casting of that stockholders' _____.

27. A summary _____ report, a condensed report, omits much of the financial information typically included in an _____ report.

28. The efficient market hypothesis relates to the ability of _____ markets to generate prices for securities that reflect _____.

29. In an efficient market, the method of _____ is not as important as whether or not the item is _____.

30. Ethics and _____ are synonymous.

31. With the expansion of international business and global capital markets, the business community and governments have shown an increased interest in the _____ of international accounting _____.

32. Financial statements of _____ separate entities may be issued to show financial position, income, and cash flow as they would appear if the companies were a single _____ (consolidated).

33. The financial statements of the parent and the _____ are consolidated for all _____ - _____ subsidiaries unless _____ is temporary or does not rest with the _____ owner.

34. With the _____ _____, the recorded assets and liabilities of the firms involved are carried forward to the combined entity at their previous recorded _____.

35. With the purchase method the firm doing the acquiring records the identifiable assets and liabilities at _____ value at the _____ of acquisition.

## Chapter 2 - Problem 2 - Multiple Choice

Choose the best answer for each of the following questions and enter the identifying letter in the space provided.

_____ 1. Which party has the primary responsibility for the financial statements?

     a. bookkeeper
     b. auditor
     c. management
     d. cost accountant
     e. none of the above

_____ 2. Which of the following is a type of audit opinion that a firm would usually prefer?

     a. unqualified opinion
     b. qualified opinion
     c. adverse opinion
     d. clear opinion
     e. none of the above

_____ 3. Which of the following statements is true?

     a. You are likely to regard an adverse opinion as an immaterial issue as to the reliability of the financial statements.
     b. A disclaimer of opinion indicates that you should look to the auditor's report as an indication of the reliability of the statements.
     c. A review is substantially more limited in scope than an examination in accordance with generally accepted auditing statements.
     d. In some cases, outside accountants are associated with financial statements when they have performed less than an audit.
     e. none of the above.

_____ 4. This item need **not** be provided with a complete set of
financial statements:

a. a twenty-year summary of operations
b. footnote disclosure of such items as accounting
policies
c. balance sheet
d. income statement
e. statement of cash flows

_____ 5. If liabilities total $60,000 and stockholders' equity
totals $40,000, then total assets are:

a. $20,000
b. $100,000
c. $60,000
d. $40,000
e. none of the above

_____ 6. Which is a permanent account?

a. land
b. moving expense
c. management expense
d. dividends
e. none of the above

_____ 7. Which is a temporary account?

a. accounts receivable
b. common stock
c. advertising expense
d. accounts payable
e. none of the above

_____ 8. In terms of debits and credits, which accounts have
the same normal balances?

a. accounts receivable, notes payable, common stock
b. dividends, notes receivable, expenses
c. dividends, notes payable, notes receivable
d. expenses, revenues, common stock
e. none of the above

_____ 9.  Frost Company had retained earnings of $30,000 at the
            end of last year.  For the current year, income was
            $15,000 and dividends $10,000.  What is the balance in
            retained earnings at the end of the current year?

            a.  $20,000
            b.  $ 5,000
            c.  $35,000
            d.  $55,000
            e.  none of the above

_____ 10. Rudd Company had retained earnings of $50,000 at the
            end of the current year.  For the current year, income
            was $20,000 and dividends $5,000.  What was the
            balance in retained earnings at the end of the prior
            year?

            a.  $50,000
            b.  $65,000
            c.  $10,000
            d.  $35,000
            e.  none of the above

_____11.  Which of the following statements is not true?

            a.  Transactions must be recorded in a journal.
            b.  All transactions could be recorded in the general
                journal.
            c.  A transaction recorded in a journal is referred to
                as a journal entry.
            d.  Accounts store the monetary information from the
                recording of transactions.
            e.  Assets, liabilities, and stockholders' equity
                accounts are referred to as temporary accounts.

Chapter 2 - Problem 3 - True/False

Indicate whether each of the following is true (T) or false (F) in the space provided.

_____ 1. Subsequent events are those events that occur after the issuance of the financial statements.

_____ 2. A disclaimer of opinion is necessary where the exceptions to fair presentation are immaterial.

_____ 3. The primary responsibility for the preparation and integrity of financial statements rests with the auditors.

_____ 4. For the balance sheet at any point in time, the assets must equal the liabilities.

_____ 5. The retained earnings account is the link between the balance sheet and the income statement.

_____ 6. A summary annual report is a condensed annual report that includes most of the financial information included in a typical annual report.

_____ 7. The major financial statements of a corporation are the balance sheet, income statement, and statement of cash flows.

_____ 8. The purpose of a balance sheet is to show the financial condition of an accounting entity for a particular period of time.

_____ 9. An income statement is a summary of revenues and expenses and gains and losses, ending with net income for a particular period of time.

_____ 10. Retained earnings is reduced by declared dividends to stockholders.

_____ 11. An estimated loss from a contingent liability should be charged to income and established as a liability only if the loss is considered probable and the amount is reasonably determinable.

_____ 12. Subsequent events are those that occur after the balance sheet date, but before the statements are issued.

_____ 13. The sequence of accounting procedures completed during each accounting period is called the accounting cycle.

_____ 14. All transactions must be recorded in the general journal.

_____ 15. The form of journals is standard from industry to industry.

_____ 16. With double-entry, each transaction is recorded with the total dollar amount of the debits equal to the total dollar amount of the credits.

_____ 17. An auditor's report is the formal presentation of all the effort that goes into an audit.

_____ 18. The auditor=s opinion states that the financial statements do not present fairly the financial position, results of operations, and cash flows of the entity in conformity with generally accepted accounting principles.

_____ 19. From the point of view of analysis, the qualified opinion without an explanatory paragraph or explanatory language carries the highest degree of reliability.

_____ 20. You are likely to regard a qualified opinion or an adverse opinion as casting serious doubts on the reliability of the financial statements.

_____ 21. The auditor will issue a qualified opinion when he/she has not performed an audit sufficient in scope to form an opinion.

_____ 22. Do not place reliance on the accountant's report for financial statements that have been compiled.

_____ 23. The responsibility for the preparation and integrity of financial statements rests with management.

_____ 24. The 10-K report is not available to the public.

_____ 25. A professional organization may formulate a code of ethics that represents a statement of aspirations and a standard of integrity beyond that required by law.

_____ 26. IASC is one of many private sector organizations involved in setting international accounting standards.

_____ 27. It is generally recognized that the market is more efficient when dealing with large firms trading on large organized stock markets than it is for small firms that are not trading on large organized stock markets.

_____ 28. It is not necessary that the market have access to relevant information.

# Chapter 2 - Problem 4 - Matching Terms Related to Financial Statements

Listed below are several terms related to financial statements. Match the letter that goes with each term.

a.   balance sheet
b.   income statement
c.   statement of retained earnings (reconciliation of retained earnings)
d.   statement of cash flows
e.   footnotes

_____   1.   Used to present additional information on items included in the financial statements and to present additional financial information.

_____   2.   Shows the financial condition of an accounting entity as of a particular date.

_____   3.   Details the inflows and outflows of cash during a specified period of time.

_____   4.   Summarizes the results of operations for a particular period of time.

_____   5.   Links the balance sheet to the income statement.

# Chapter 2 - Problem 5 - Matching Terms

Listed below are several terms. Match the letter that goes with each term.

a.  sole proprietorship  
b.  partnership  
c.  business corporation  
d.  contingent liabilities  
e.  subsequent events  
f.  accounting cycle  

g.  transaction  
h.  accounting equation  
i.  permanent accounts  
j.  temporary accounts  
k.  proxy  
l.  summary annual report  

_____ 1.  The solicitation sent to stockholders for the election of directors and for the approval of other corporation actions.

_____ 2.  The balances in these accounts carry forward to the next accounting period.

_____ 3.  Assets = Liabilities + Stockholders' Equity

_____ 4.  Liabilities that may result in payment, depending on a particular occurrence such as settlement of litigation or the ruling of the tax court.

_____ 5.  Events that occur after the balance sheet date, but before the statements are issued.

_____ 6.  The sequence of accounting procedures completed during each accounting period.

_____ 7.  A business owned by one person is not a legal entity separate from its owner.

_____ 8.  A condensed report that omits much of the financial information typically included in an annual report.

_____ 9.  Accounts closed to retained earnings and not carried into the next period.

_____ 10.  A business owned by two or more individuals. Each owner is personally responsible for the debts of the business.

_____ 11.  An event that causes a change in a company's assets, liabilities, or stockholders' equity.

_____ 12.  A legal entity incorporated in a particular state.

Chapter 2 - Problem 6 - Identification of Accounts as Permanent
                        or Temporary and Identification of Normal Balance

Listed below are several accounts.  In the space provided (1)
indicate the account as a permanent (P) or temporary (T) account,
and (2) indicate the normal balance in terms of debit (Dr) or
credit (Cr).

|                      | Permanent (P) or Temporary (T) | Normal Balance Dr (Cr) |
| Account              |                                |                        |
|----------------------|--------------------------------|------------------------|
| Notes receivable     | _____                          | _____                  |
| Land                 | _____                          | _____                  |
| Patent               | _____                          | _____                  |
| Wages payable        | _____                          | _____                  |
| Common stock         | _____                          | _____                  |
| Revenue              | _____                          | _____                  |
| Advertising expense  | _____                          | _____                  |
| Wages expense        | _____                          | _____                  |
| Retained earnings    | _____                          | _____                  |
| Inventory            | _____                          | _____                  |

Chapter 2 - Problem 7 - Identification of Financial Statement

Listed below are several accounts or statement categories.  In
the space provided indicate the financial statement as balance
sheet (BS), income statement (IS), or statement of cash flows
(SCF).

|                                      | Balance Sheet (BS) Income Statement (IS) Statement of Cash Flows (SCF) |
| Account Statement Category           |                                                                        |
|--------------------------------------|------------------------------------------------------------------------|
| Cash                                 | _____                                                          |
| Liabilities                          | _____                                                          |
| Other assets                         | _____                                                          |
| Accounts payable                     | _____                                                          |
| Retained earnings                    | _____                                                          |
| Salaries expense                     | _____                                                          |
| Salaries payable                     | _____                                                          |
| Cash flow from operating activities  | _____                                                          |
| Sales                                | _____                                                          |
| Stockholders' equity                 | _____                                                          |
| Cash flows from investing activities | _____                                                          |
| Insurance expense                    | _____                                                          |
| Cash flow from financing activities  | _____                                                          |
| Rent expense                         | _____                                                          |
| Utility expense                      | _____                                                          |
| Assets                               | _____                                                          |
| Revenues                             | _____                                                          |

Chapter 2 - Problem 8 - Identification of Auditor's Report

Below is a list of auditor's reports as well as a list of phrases describing the reports.  In the space provided, place the appropriate letter identifying each type of auditor's report.

    a.  unqualified
    b.  qualified
    c.  adverse
    d.  disclaimer
    e.  reviewed
    f.  compiled

_____ 1.  Consists principally of inquiries made to company personnel and analytical procedures applied to financial data.

_____ 2.  Presentation of financial information as presented by management.

_____ 3.  The auditor does not express an opinion on the financial statements.

_____ 4.  This opinion states that, except for the effects of the matter(s) to which the qualification relates, the financial statements present fairly, in all material respects, the financial position, results of operations, and cash flows of the entity in conformity with generally accepted accounting principles.

_____ 5.  This opinion states that the financial statements present fairly, in all material respects, the financial position, results of operations, and cash flows of the entity, in conformity with generally accepted accounting principles.

_____ 6.  This opinion states that the financial statements do not present fairly the financial position, results of operations, and cash flows of the entity in conformity with generally accepted accounting principles.

# Chapter 2 - Problem 9 - Record the Transactions Using T-Accounts

Record the following transactions, using T-accounts.

1. Cash sales of $10,000
2. Credit sales of $20,000
3. Collected $2,000 on accounts receivable
4. Bought equipment that cost $5,000 on credit (accounts payable)
5. Collected $3,000 on an account receivable
6. Sold common stock for $10,000 cash
7. Paid $2,000 on accounts payable

# Chapter 2 - Problem 10 - Record the Adjusting Entries Using T-Accounts

Using the information provided record the following adjusting entries using T-accounts.  Assume that the accounting year ends on December 31.

1.   Salaries payable in the amount of $500 have not been recorded at December 31.

2.   $2,000 paid for insurance on July 1 for a one-year period (July 1 - June 30).  This transaction was recorded as a debit to Insurance Expense ($2,000) and a credit T-Cash ($2,000).

3.   Rent expense in the amount of $800 was paid on December 1. This transaction was recorded as a debit to rent expense ($800) and a credit to cash ($800).  This rent payment was for a two month period (December and January).

4.   Interest on notes payable in the amount of $300 has not been recorded at December 31.

## CHAPTER 2 - SOLUTIONS

Chapter 2 - Problem 1 - Supply the Words Necessary to Complete
     the Following Items

1.  corporation

2.  owners' equity

3.  date

4.  links; income statement

5.  period of time

6.  period of time

7.  investing activities; financing activities

8.  footnotes; financial

9.  contingent liabilities

10.  subsequent events

11.  transaction; financial position

12.  special; general journal

13.  transactions; general ledger

14.  transaction; debits; credits

15.  left; right

16.  permanent accounts; period

17.  temporary accounts; retained earnings

18.  accrual basis; income statement

19.  income; balance sheet

20.  auditor's report; audit

21.  unqualified opinion; reliability

22.  review; procedures

23. audited; reviewed

24. auditor; opinion; audit

25. 45; quarter

26. proxy; vote

27. annual; annual

28. capital; worth

29. disclosure; disclosed

30. morals

31. harmonization; standards

32. legally; entity

33. subsidiary; majority-owned; control; majority

34. pooling method; amounts

35. fair; date

Chapter 2 - Problem 2 - Multiple Choice

__c__  1. The responsibility for the preparation and integrity of financial statements rests with management.

__a__  2. This opinion states that the financial statements present fairly, in all material respects, the financial position, results of operations, and cash flows of the entity, in conformity with GAAP.

__d__  3. The accountants may have performed a review or compiled the financial statements.

__a__  4. There is no requirement for a twenty-year summary of operations.

__b__  5. Assets = Liabilities + Stockholders' Equity
       Assets = $60,000      +         $40,000
       Assets = $100,000

__a__  6. Asset, liability, and stockholders' equity accounts are referred to as permanent accounts because the balances in these accounts carry forward to the next accounting period.

__c__  7. Balances in revenue, expense, gain, loss, and dividend accounts, described as temporary accounts, are closed to retained earnings and not carried into the next period.

__b__  8. Dividends, notes receivable, and expenses have a normal debit balance.

__c__  9. Retained earnings, end of last year          $30,000
          Income                                        15,000
          Dividends                                    (10,000)
          Retained earnings, end of current year       $35,000

__d__ 10. Retained earnings, end of last year                x
          Income                                        20,000
          Dividends                                    ( 5,000)
          Retained earnings, end of current year       $50,000

39

<u>  e  </u> 11. Assets, liabilities, and stockholders' equity accounts
                are referred to as permanent accounts.

## Chapter 2 - Problem 3 - True/False

| | | | | | | | |
|---|---|---|---|---|---|---|---|
| F | 1. | T | 10. | F | 19. | F | 28. |
| F | 2. | T | 11. | T | 20. | | |
| F | 3. | T | 12. | F | 21. | | |
| F | 4. | T | 13. | T | 22. | | |
| T | 5. | F | 14. | T | 23. | | |
| F | 6. | F | 15. | F | 24. | | |
| T | 7. | T | 16. | T | 25. | | |
| F | 8. | T | 17. | F | 26. | | |
| T | 9. | F | 18. | T | 27. | | |

## Chapter 2 - Problem 4 - Matching Terms Related to Financial Statements

| | | | |
|---|---|---|---|
| e | 1. | b | 4. |
| a | 2. | c | 5. |
| d | 3. | | |

## Chapter 2 - Problem 5 - Matching Terms

| | | | |
|---|---|---|---|
| k | 1. | a | 7. |
| i | 2. | l | 8. |
| h | 3. | j | 9. |
| d | 4. | b | 10. |
| e | 5. | g | 11. |
| f | 6. | c | 12. |

## Chapter 2 - Problem 6 - Identification of Accounts as Permanent or Temporary and Identification of Normal Balance

| Account | Permanent (P) or Temporary (T) | Normal Balance Dr (Cr.) |
|---|---|---|
| Notes receivable | P | Dr. |
| Land | P | Dr. |
| Patent | P | Dr. |
| Wages payable | P | Cr. |
| Common stock | P | Cr. |
| Revenue | T | Cr. |
| Advertising expense | T | Dr. |
| Wages expense | T | Dr. |
| Retained earnings | P | Cr. |
| Inventory | P | Dr. |

# Chapter 2 - Problem 7 - Identification of Financial Statement and Identification of Normal Balance

| Account or Statement Category | Balance Sheet (BS) Income Statement (IS) Statement of Cash Flows (SCF) |
|---|---|
| Cash | BS |
| Liabilities | BS |
| Other assets | BS |
| Accounts payable | BS |
| Retained earnings | BS |
| Salaries expense | IS |
| Salaries payable | BS |
| Cash flow from operating activities | SCF |
| Sales | IS |
| Cash flows from investing activities | SCF |
| Insurance expense | IS |
| Stockholders' equity | BS |
| Cash flows from financing activities | SCF |
| Rent expense | IS |
| Utility expense | IS |
| Assets | BS |
| Revenue | IS |

## Chapter 2 - Problem 8 - Identification of Auditor's Report

| | |
|---|---|
| e | 1. |
| f | 2. |
| d | 3. |
| b | 4. |
| a | 5. |
| c | 6. |

## Chapter 2 - Problem 9 - Record the Transactions Using T-Accounts

### Cash

| | |
|---|---|
| (1) 10,000 | (7) 2,000 |
| (3)  2,000 | |
| (5)  3,000 | |
| (6) 10,000 | |

### Sales

| | |
|---|---|
| | (1) 10,000 |
| | (2) 20,000 |

### Accounts Receivable

| | |
|---|---|
| (2) 20,000 | (3) 2,000 |
| | (5) 3,000 |

### Accounts Payable

| | |
|---|---|
| (7) 2,000 | (4) 5,000 |

### Equipment

| | |
|---|---|
| (4) 5,000 | |

### Common Stock

| | |
|---|---|
| | (6) 10,000 |

# Chapter 2 - Problem 10 - Record the Adjusting Entries Using T-Accounts

|                | Salaries Expense |                |          | Salaries Payable |                |
|----------------|------------------|----------------|----------|------------------|----------------|
| (1) 500        |                  |                |          |                  | (1) 500        |

|                | Insurance Expense |               |          | Prepaid Insurance |               |
|----------------|-------------------|---------------|----------|-------------------|---------------|
|                |                   | (2) 1,000     | (2) 1,000 |                  |               |

|                | Rent Expense      |               |          | Prepaid Rent      |               |
|----------------|-------------------|---------------|----------|-------------------|---------------|
|                |                   | (3) 400       | (3) 400  |                   |               |

|                | Interest Expense  |               |          | Interest Payable  |               |
|----------------|-------------------|---------------|----------|-------------------|---------------|
| (4) 300        |                   |               |          |                   | (4) 300       |

# Chapter 3:  Balance Sheet

Chapter 3 - Problem 1 - Supply the Words Necessary to Complete
                     the Following Items

1.  A balance sheet shows the financial _____ of an
    accounting entity as of a particular _____.

2.  At any point in time, the assets must _____ the
    contribution of the _____ and owners.

3.  Assets are probable future _____ benefits obtained or
    _____ by an entity as a result of past transactions or
    events.

4.  The operating cycle covers the time between the acquisition
    of _____ and the realization of _____ from selling the
    inventory.

5.  When a significant _____ is consolidated from an industry
    that does not use the concept of _____ and _____, then
    the consolidated statements will not use the concept of
    current and noncurrent.

6.  Current assets are listed on the balance sheet in order of
    _____.

7.  Cash, the most liquid asset, includes negotiable checks and
    _____ balances in checking accounts, as well as cash on
    hand.

8.  Marketable securities are characterized by their _____ at
    a readily determinable _____ price.

9.  The carrying basis of debt and equity marketable securities
    is ____ value.

10. _____ _____ are monies due on accounts that arise from
    sales or services rendered to customers.

11. Inventories in a manufacturing firm include raw materials,
    work in process, and _____ _____.

12. Inventories will be carried at ____, expressed in terms of
    lower-of-cost-or-_____.

13. Since retailing and wholesaling firms do not engage in the manufacture of a product but only in the sale, their only inventory item is _____.

14. A _____ is an expenditure made in advance of the use of the service or goods.

15. Long-term assets are usually divided into four categories: tangible assets, _____, _____ assets, and other.

16. Construction in progress represents cost incurred for projects _____ _____.

17. _____ is the process of allocating the ____ of buildings and machinery over the periods benefited.

18. Often a firm depreciates an asset under one method for _____ _____ and another for income ___ returns.

19. Over the life of an asset, the total depreciation will be the _____ regardless of the depreciation _____ selected.

20. The declining-balance depreciation method applies a _____ times the straight-line rate to the declining _____ value.

21. The sum-of-the-years'-digits depreciation method takes a _____ each year times the ____.

22. If the lease is in substance an ownership arrangement, it is a _____ lease; otherwise, the lease is an _____ lease.

23. Long-term investments, usually stocks and bonds of other companies, are often held to maintain a _____ relationship or to exercise _____.

24. Intangibles are recorded at _____ _____ and amortized over their _____ lives or their legal lives, whichever is _____.

25. Goodwill arises from the acquisition of a business for a sum _____ than the physical asset value, usually because the business has unusual earning _____.

26. Liabilities are _____ future sacrifices of economic benefits arising from present obligations of a particular entity to transfer assets or provide services to other entities in the _____ as a result of past transactions or _____.

27. Current liabilities are obligations whose liquidation is reasonably expected to require the use of existing current _____ or the creation of other current _____ within a ____ or operating cycle, whichever is _____.

28. Long-term liabilities are those due in a period exceeding ____ year or one operating cycle, whichever is _____.

29. Minority interest reflects the ownership of _____ shareholders in the equity of consolidated subsidiaries ____ than wholly owned.

30. Redeemable preferred stock is subject to _____ redemption requirements or has a redemption feature outside the _____ of this issue.

31. Stockholders' equity is the residual ownership interest in the _____ of an entity that remains after deducting its _____.

32. _____ stock shares in all the stockholders' rights and represents ownership that has _____ and liquidation rights.

33. _____ stock seldom has voting right.

34. _____ capital is donated to the company by stockholders', creditors, or other parties.

35. Retained earnings are the undistributed _____ of the corporation.

36. A _____-_____ is an accounting procedure equivalent to an accounting fresh start.

37. Conceptually, accumulated other comprehensive income represents _____ _____ from other comprehensive income.

38.  An _____ is a qualified stock-bonus, or combination stock-bonus and money-purchase pension plan, designed to invest primarily in the employer's _____.

39.  A firm creates _____ _____ when it repurchases its own stock and does not _____ it.

40.  A statement of stockholders' equity represents a reconciliation of the _____ and _____ balances of their stockholder accounts.


## Chapter 3 - Problem 2 - Multiple Choice

Choose the best answer for each of the following questions and enter the identifying letter in the space provided.

_____  1.  Which of the following would **not** appear on a conventional balance sheet?

   a.  accounts receivable
   b.  accounts payable
   c.  patents
   d.  gain from sale of land
   e.  common stock

_____  2.  Current assets typically include all but one of the following assets:

   a.  cash restricted for the retirement of bonds.
   b.  unrestricted cash.
   c.  marketable securities.
   d.  receivables.
   e.  inventories.

_____  3.  The current liabilities section of the balance sheet should include:

   a.  land.
   b.  cash surrender value of life insurance.
   c.  accounts payable.
   d.  bonds payable.
   e.  preferred stock.

_____ 4. Inventories are the balance of goods on hand. In a manufacturing firm, they include all but one of the following:

   a. raw material.
   b. work in process.
   c. finished goods.
   d. supplies.
   e. land.

_____ 5. Which of the following accounts would **not** usually be classified as a current liability?

   a. accounts payable
   b. wages payable
   c. unearned rent income
   d. bonds payable
   e. taxes payable

_____ 6. Where should redeemable preferred stock be classified for analysis purposes?

   a. marketable security
   b. long-term investment
   c. intangible
   d. liabilities
   e. shareholders' equity

_____ 7. Which of the following accounts would **not** be classified as an intangible?

   a. goodwill
   b. patent
   c. accounts receivable
   d. trademarks
   e. franchises

_____ 8. Growth Company had total assets of $100,000 and total liabilities of $60,000. What is the balance of the stockholders' equity?

   a. $0
   b. $40,000
   c. $60,000
   d. $100,000
   e. none of the above

_____ 9. The current asset section of the balance sheet should include:

    a. inventory.
    b. taxes payable.
    c. land.
    d. patents.
    e. bonds payable.

_____ 10. Which of the following is **not** a typical current liability?

    a. accounts payable
    b. wages payable
    c. interest payable
    d. pension liabilities
    e. taxes payable

_____ 11. Which of the following is a current liability?

    a. unearned rent income
    b. prepaid interest
    c. land
    d. common stock
    e. none of the above

_____ 12. Company A owns shares of Company B. Company A reports "Minority Interest" on its balance sheet. This account represents:

    a. the minority share by outside owners of the stock of B.
    b. A's minority share of the stock of B.
    c. the minority share by outside owners of the stock of A.
    d. the majority interest in A.
    e. none of the above.

_____ 13. Treasury stock is best classified as:

    a. a current liability.
    b. a current asset.
    c. a reduction of stockholders' equity.
    d. a contra asset.
    e. a contra liability.

_____ 14. A company owns shares of voting stock in another company. When would the subsidiary company data be consolidated with the company?

a. When the company owns 30% of the subsidiary.
b. The financial statements of the parent and the subsidiary are usually consolidated for all majority-owned subsidiaries.
c. When the company has substantial influence on the subsidiary.
d. When the company owns 20% of the stock of the subsidiary and has substantial influence.
e. When the company owns 20% of the stock of the subsidiary but does not have substantial influence.

_____ 15. When a subsidiary is **not** consolidated, then it is accounted for on the parent's balance sheet as:

a. marketable security.
b. investment.
c. other asset.
d. minority interest.
e. fixed asset.

_____ 16. When an ESOP borrows funds and the firm commits to future contributions to the ESOP to meet the debt-service requirements, the firm records this commitment as:

a. a liability and as a deduction from stockholders' equity.
b. a liability and an asset.
c. an increase in stockholders' equity.
d. a decrease in liabilities.
e. none of the above.

_____ 17. Which of the following would **not** usually be considered as an advantage of an ESOP from the perspective of the firm?

a. A significant amount of voting stock in the hands of employees.
b. Help in financing a leveraged buyout.
c. Help in creating a market for the company's stock.
d. Source of funds at a reasonable rate.
e. None of the above.

Chapter 3 - Problem 3 - True/False

Indicate whether each of the following is true (T) or false (F) in the space provided.

_____  1.  The purpose of a balance sheet is to show the financial condition of an accounting entity for a period of time.

_____  2.  The balance sheet is presented with the assets equal to liabilities plus equity.  When this presentation is presented side by side, it is called the report format.

_____  3.  Generally accepted accounting principles require a specific format for the presentation of a balance sheet.

_____  4.  The analyst must assume that securities classified as marketable securities are readily marketable.

_____  5.  Accounts receivable are usually carried at an amount that is expected to be collected.

_____  6.  Generally accepted accounting principles and the Internal Revenue Code of tax law allow for one method of depreciation for tax purposes and another for reporting purposes.

_____  7.  The amount of tax expense is based on reported income; the actual tax payable is computed from taxable income.  When tax expense is greater than taxes payable, then the deferred tax credit account is increased.

_____  8.  From the standpoint of the lessee, if the lease is in substance an ownership arrangement, it will be a capital lease; otherwise, the lease will be an operating lease.

_____  9.  Subsidiaries that have been consolidated will be disclosed under investments.

_____ 10.  Intangibles are generally amortized over their useful lives or their legal lives, whichever is longer.

_____ 11.  Minority interest reflects the ownership of minority shareholders in the equity of consolidated subsidiaries that are less than wholly-owned.

_____ 12.  Treasury stock represents an increase in paid-in capital.

_____ 13. All items of value to a firm are included as assets.

_____ 14. The employer contribution to an ESOP is charged to expense on the income statement.

_____ 15. Minority interest reflects the ownership of minority shareholders in the equity of unconsolidated subsidiaries that are less than wholly-owned.

_____ 16. When a firm repurchases its own stock and does not retire it, the stock is called treasury stock.

_____ 17. When a subsidiary is consolidated, then it is accounted for as an investment on the parent's balance sheet.

_____ 18. All assets are normally divided into current assets and investments.

_____ 19. Some industries do not divide assets (or liabilities) into current and noncurrent.

_____ 20. Under the equity method of carrying an investment, the cost is adjusted for the proportionate share of the rise (fall) in retained profits of the subsidiary (investee).

_____ 21. Goodwill arises from the acquisition of a business for a sum less than the physical asset value.

_____ 22. Long-term liabilities are those due in a period exceeding one year or one operating cycle, whichever is shorter.

## Chapter 3 - Problem 4 - Balance Sheet Classification

Assume that Oregon Pop Corp. uses the following headings on its balance sheet:

A.  Current assets
B.  Investments
C.  Property, plant, and
    and equipment
D.  Intangible assets

E.  Current liabilities
F.  Long-term liabilities
G.  Capital stock
H.  Paid-in capital in
    excess of par
I.  Retained earnings

Indicate by letter how each of the following should be best classified. If an item would not appear on the balance sheet, but would appear in a footnote to the financial statements, use the letter "N" to indicate this fact. If an item is not reported on the balance sheet, use the letter "X". If the account balance is normally opposite that of a typical account in that classification, indicate this by placing the letter in parentheses, ( ).

_____ 1.  Marketable securities

_____ 2.  Long-term debt due within one year

_____ 3.  Investments in affiliated companies not consolidated

_____ 4.  Patents

_____ 5.  Trademarks

_____ 6.  Buildings, machinery, and equipment, net

_____ 7.  Long-term debt due after one year

_____ 8.  Preferred stock of no par value

_____ 9.  Prepaid expenses

_____ 10.  Wages and salaries payable

_____ 11.  Land

_____ 12.  Inventories

_____ 13.  Accumulated deficit

_____ 14.  Accumulated depreciation

_____ 15.  Cash dividend payable

# Chapter 3 - Problem 5 - Matching Balance Sheet Classifications

Listed below are several balance sheet classifications. Match
the letter that goes with each classification.

a.  current assets
b.  long-term assets
c.  tangible assets
d.  investments
e.  intangibles
f.  current liabilities
g.  long-term liabilities
h.  owners' equity

_____ 1.  The residual ownership interest in the assets of an
            entity that remains after deducting its liabilities.

_____ 2.  Obligations whose liquidation is reasonably expected
            to require the use of existing current assets or the
            creation of other current liabilities within a year or
            an operating cycle, whichever is longer.

_____ 3.  Noncurrent assets that take longer than a year or an
            operating cycle to be converted to cash or to conserve
            cash.

_____ 4.  Assets that are listed on the balance sheet in order
            of liquidity.

_____ 5.  The physical facilities used in the operations of the
            business.

_____ 6.  Nonphysical assets, such as patents and copyrights.

_____ 7.  Usually stocks and bonds of other companies, often
            held to maintain a business relationship or exercise
            control.

_____ 8.  Liabilities due in a period exceeding one year or one
            operating cycle, whichever is longer.

# Chapter 3 - Problem 6 - Matching Definition of Specific Accounts

Listed below are several account titles.  Match the letter that
goes with each definition.

a.   cash                             n.   buildings
b.   accounts receivable             o.   accumulated depreciation
c.   land                            p.   patent
d.   machinery                       q.   organizational costs
e.   goodwill                        r.   franchises
f.   trademarks                      s.   notes payable
g.   accounts payable                t.   preferred stock
h.   redeemable preferred stock      u.   retained earnings
i.   minority interest               v.   donated capital
j.   common stock                    w.   supplies
k.   marketable securities           x.   finished goods
l.   inventories                     y.   work in process
m.   prepaid insurance               z.   raw material

_____  1.   The undistributed earnings of the corporation.

_____  2.   Capital donated to the company by stockholders,
              creditors, or other parties.

_____  3.   Stock that shares in all of the stockholders' rights
              and represents ownership that has voting and
              liquidation rights.

_____  4.   The most liquid asset, includes negotiable checks and
              unrestricted balances in checking accounts, as well as
              cash on hand.

_____  5.   Monies due on accounts from customers arise from sales
              or services rendered.

_____  6.   Arises from the acquisition of a business for a sum
              greater than the physical asset value, usually because
              the business has unusual earning power.

_____  7.   Short-term obligations created by the acquisition of
              goods and services.

_____  8.   Reflects the ownership of minority shareholders in the
              equity of consolidated subsidiaries less than wholly
              owned.

_____  9.   Preferred stock subject to mandatory redemption
              requirements, or has a redemption feature outside the
              control of the issuer.

_____ 10.   The balance of goods on hand.

_____ 11. Is shown at acquisition cost and is not depreciated because it does not get used up.

_____ 12. Names or symbols where rights are granted to the holder for ten years, with an option for renewal.

_____ 13. Characterized by their marketability at a readily determinable market price; can be readily converted into cash.

_____ 14. An insurance expenditure made in advance.

_____ 15. Structures presented at cost plus the cost of permanent improvements.

_____ 16. A contra asset that is subtracted from the cost of plant and equipment.

_____ 17. The legal costs incurred when a business is organized.

_____ 18. Stock that has one or more preferences over common stock.

_____ 19. Equipment listed at historical cost, including delivery and installation, plus any material improvements that extend its life or increase the quantity or quality of service.

_____ 20. The legal right to operate under a particular corporate name, providing trade-name products or services.

_____ 21. Exclusive legal rights granted to an inventor for a period of twenty years, and valued at their acquisition cost.

_____ 22. Promissory notes due in the future.

_____ 23. A type of inventory used indirectly in the production of goods or services.

_____ 24. Inventory of a manufacturing firm ready for sale.

_____ 25. Inventory of a manufacturing firm in process but not ready for sale.

_____ 26. Inventory of a manufacturing firm purchased for direct use in manufacturing a product, and they become part of the product.

# Chapter 3 - Problem 7 - Balance Sheet Presentation

A partial list of accounts for Grayson Company is presented below:

Cash
Interest expense
Long-term investment
Selling expense
Sales
Land
Redeemable preferred stock
Other income
Cash equivalents
Income taxes currently payable
Other assets - long-term
Administrative expenses
Cost of goods sold
Accounts receivable
Short-term notes receivable
Current portion of long-term debt
Minority interest
Common stock
Inventories
Retained earnings
Accounts payable
Accrued salaries
Prepaid expenses
Minority interest in subsidiaries' earnings
Common stock held in treasury, at cost
Other current liabilities
Buildings
Long-term debt
Equipment
Construction in progress
Accumulated depreciation

**Required:** Prepare a balance sheet without monetary amounts for December 31, 20XX, using the format provided.

Grayson Company
Balance Sheet
December 31, 20XX

Assets
Current assets:

Total current assets
Property, plant, and equipment:

Net property, plant and equipment

Investments:

Other:

Total assets

Liabilities and stockholders' equity
Current liabilities:

Total current liabilities

Stockholders' equity:

Total stockholders' equity

Total liabilities and stockholders' equity

# Chapter 3 - Problem 8 - Depreciation Computation

An item of equipment acquired on January 1 at a cost of $50,000 has an estimated life of five years. Assume that the equipment will have a salvage value of $5,000. It has an estimated use of 20,000 hours. The actual use was 6,000 hours (year 1); 4,000 hours (year 2); 4,000 hours (year 3); 3,000 hours (year 4); and 5,000 hours (year 5).

**Required:** Determine the depreciation for the first three years by the following methods:

a. straight-line
b. double declining balance
c. sum-of-the-years'-digits
d. unit of production

Dean Company has had 4,000 shares of 8%, $100 par-value preferred stock and 24,000 shares of $5 par-value common stock outstanding for the last two years. During the most recent year, dividends paid totaled $50,000; in the prior year, dividends paid totaled $25,000.

**Required:** Compute the amount of dividends that must have been paid to preferred stockholders and common stockholders in each of the years, given the following independent assumptions:

    a.     Preferred stock is fully participating
    b.     Preferred stock is cumulative
    c.     Preferred stock participates up to 5% of its par value
    d.     Preferred stock is nonparticipating and noncumulative

## CHAPTER 3 - SOLUTIONS

Chapter 3 - Problem 1 - Supply the Words Necessary to Complete the Following Items

1. condition; date

2. equal; creditors

3. economic; controlled

4. inventory; cash

5. subsidiary; current; noncurrent

6. liquidity

7. unrestricted

8. marketability; market

9. fair

10. Accounts receivable

11. finished goods

12. cost; market

13. merchandise

14. prepaid

15. investments; intangible

16. under construction

17. Depreciation; cost

18. financial statements; tax

19. same; method

20. multiple; book

21. fraction; cost

22. capital; operating

23. business; control

24. historical cost; useful; shorter

25. greater; power

26. probable; future; events

27. assets; liabilities; year; longer

28. one; longer

29. minority; less

30. mandatory; control

31. assets; liabilities

32. Common; voting

33. Preferred

34. Donated

35. earnings

36. quasi-reorganization

37. retained earnings

38. ESOP; securities

39. treasury stock; retire

40. beginning; ending

# Chapter 3 - Problem 2 - Multiple Choice

__d__  1. The income statement summarizes revenues and expenses and gains and losses, ending with net income.

__a__  2. The definition of current assets excludes restricted cash.

__c__  3. Current liabilities are obligations whose liquidation is reasonably expected to require the use of existing current assets or the creation of other current liabilities within a year or an operating cycle, whichever is longer.  This would include accounts payable.

__e__  4. Inventories are the balance of goods on hand.  In a manufacturing firm, they include raw materials, work in process, finished goods, and supplies.

__d__  5. Current liabilities are obligations whose liquidation is reasonably expected to require the use of existing current assets or the creation of other current liabilities within a year or an operating cycle, whichever is longer.  Bonds payable are financing arrangements that usually do not meet this definition.

__d__  6. Redeemable preferred stock, non-redeemable preferred stock, and common stock are not to be totaled in the balance sheet.  Further, the stockholders' equity section should not include redeemable preferred stock. Because redeemable preferred stock is more like debt than equity, consider it as part of total liabilities.

__c__  7. Under generally accepted accounting principles accounts receivable are not classified as an intangible.

__b__  8. Assets     = Liabilities + Owners' Equity
$100,000 = $60,000      + ?
$100,000 - $60,000 = $40,000

__a__  9. Current assets are assets (1) in the form of cash, (2) that will normally be realized in cash, or (3) that conserve the use of cash during the operating cycle of a firm or for one year, whichever is longer. Inventory meets this definition.

d    10. Current liabilities are obligations whose liquidation is reasonably expected to require the use of existing current assets or the creation of other current liabilities within a year or an operating cycle, whichever is longer. Pension liabilities do not usually meet this definition.

a    11. Current liabilities are obligations whose liquidation is reasonably expected to require the use of existing current assets or the creation of other current liabilities within a year or an operating cycle, whichever is longer. Unearned rent income meets this definition.

a    12. Minority interest reflects the ownership of minority shareholders in the equity of consolidated subsidiaries less than wholly owned.

c    13. A firm creates treasury stock when it repurchases its own stock and does not retire it. Since treasury stock lowers the stock outstanding, it is subtracted from stockholders' equity.

b    14. The financial statements of the parent and the subsidiary are consolidated for all majority-owned subsidiaries, unless control is temporary or does not rest with the majority owner.

b    15. An unconsolidated subsidiary is accounted for as an investment on the parent's balance sheet.

a    16. When an ESOP borrows funds and the firm (in either an informal or formal guarantee) commits to future contributions to the ESOP to meet the debt-service requirements, then the firm records this commitment as a liability and as a deferred compensation deduction within stockholders' equity.

a    17. A significant amount of voting stock in the hands of employees would usually not be considered as an advantage of an ESOP from the perspective of the firm.

## Chapter 3 - Problem 3 - True/False

| | | | | | | | |
|---|---|---|---|---|---|---|---|
| F | 1. | T | 8. | F | 15. | F | 22. |
| F | 2. | F | 9. | T | 16. | | |
| F | 3. | F | 10. | F | 17. | | |
| T | 4. | T | 11. | F | 18. | | |
| T | 5. | F | 12. | T | 19. | | |
| T | 6. | F | 13. | T | 20. | | |
| T | 7. | T | 14. | F | 21. | | |

## Chapter 3 - Problem 4 - Balance Sheet Classification

| | | | |
|---|---|---|---|
| A | 1. | E | 10. |
| E | 2. | C | 11. |
| B | 3. | A | 12. |
| D | 4. | (I) | 13. |
| D | 5. | (C) | 14. |
| C | 6. | E | 15. |
| F | 7. | | |
| G | 8. | | |
| A | 9. | | |

## Chapter 3 - Problem 5 - Matching Balance Sheet Classifications

| | | | |
|---|---|---|---|
| h | 1. | c | 5. |
| f | 2. | e | 6. |
| b | 3. | d | 7. |
| a | 4. | g | 8. |

## Chapter 3 - Problem 6 - Matching Definition of Specific Accounts

| | | | | | |
|---|---|---|---|---|---|
| u | 1. | f | 12. | w | 23. |
| v | 2. | k | 13. | x | 24. |
| j | 3. | m | 14. | y | 25. |
| a | 4. | n | 15. | z | 26. |
| b | 5. | o | 16. | | |
| e | 6. | q | 17. | | |
| g | 7. | t | 18. | | |
| i | 8. | d | 19. | | |
| h | 9. | r | 20. | | |
| l | 10. | p | 21. | | |
| c | 11. | s | 22. | | |

# Chapter 3 - Problem 7 - Balance Sheet Presentation

## Grayson Company
## Balance Sheet
## December 31, 20XX

Assets
Current assets:
Cash
Cash equivalents
Accounts receivable
Short-term notes receivable
Inventories
Prepaid expenses
Total current assets

Property, plant, and equipment:
Land
Buildings
Equipment
Construction in progress
Less accumulated depreciation
Net property, plant, and equipment

Investments:
Long-term investment
Other:
Other assets - long-term

Total assets

Liabilities and stockholders' equity
Current liabilities:
Accounts payable
Accrued salaries
Income taxes currently payable
Current portion of long-term debt
Other current liabilities
Total current liabilities

Long-term debt
Minority interest
Redeemable preferred stock

Stockholders' equity:
Common stock
Retained earnings
Common stock held in treasury, at cost
Total stockholders' equity
Total liabilities and stockholders' equity

Chapter 3 - Problem 8 - Depreciation Computation

a.  straight-line: $\dfrac{\$50,000 - \$5,000}{5}$ = $9,000 per year

b.  double declining-balance:

Year 1:
1/5 x 2 x $50,000=$20,000

Year 2:
1/5 x 2 x ($50,000-$20,000)=$12,000

Year 3:
1/5 x 2 x ($50,000-$20,000-$12,000)= $7,200

c.  Sum-of-the-years'-digits:

5 + 4 + 3 + 2 + 1 = 15 digits

Year 1:
5/15 x ($50,000 - $5,000) = $15,000

Year 2:
4/15 x ($50,000 - $5,000) = $12,000

Year 3:
3/15 x ($50,000 - $5,000) = $ 9,000

d.  Unit of production:

Depreciation per unit hour = $\dfrac{(\$50,000 - \$5,000)}{20,000}$ = $2.25

Year 1:
6,000 x $2.25 = $13,500

Year 2:
4,000 x $2.25 = $ 9,000

Year 3:
4,000 x $2.25 = $ 9,000

Chapter 3 - Problem 9 - Allocation of Dividends

|  | | Preferred | Common |
|---|---|---|---|

a. Year 1
   Preferred
   4,000 x $100 x 8% = $32,000
   The entire $25,000 in year 1
   goes to preferred.                        $25,000       -0-

   Year 2
   Preferred
   4,000 x $100 x 8% = $32,000      $32,000

   Common
   24,000 x $5 = $120,000 x 8%
               $9,600                           $ 9,600
   Fully participating, therefore the
   remaining dividend will be split
   between preferred and common in
   proportion to their outstanding
   stock at total par value.

   Total par value
   of preferred:     $400,000    76.92%

   Total par value
   of common:       120,000     23.08%
                         $520,000    100.00%

   Remaining dividend to allocate:
   ($50,000 - $32,000 - $9,600) = $8,400

   Preferred:    76.92% x $8,400       6,461
   Common:      23.08% x $8,400                                  1,939
                                         $38,461    $11,539

|  | | Preferred | Common |
|---|---|---|---|

b.

Year 1
Preferred
4,000 x $100 x 8% = $32,000
The entire $25,000 in year 1
goes to preferred

|  | Preferred | Common |
|---|---|---|
|  | $25,000 | -0- |

$7,000 accumulates

Year 2
Preferred
Cumulative from year 1   $ 7,000
4,000 x $100 x 8% =        32,000    $39,000

Common
The remaining dividends go to
common ($50,000 - $39,000)

|  | Preferred | Common |
|---|---|---|
|  |  | 11,000 |
|  | $39,000 | $11,000 |

|  | Preferred | Common |
|---|---|---|

c.  Year 1
Preferred
4,000 x $100 x 8% =0 $32,000
The entire $25,00 in year 1
goes to preferred.

|  | Preferred | Common |
|---|---|---|
|  | $25,000 | -0- |

Year 2
Preferred
4,000 x $100 x 8% = $32,000    $32,000

Common
24,000 x $5 = $120,000 x 8% = $9,600

|  | Common |
|---|---|
|  | 9,600 |

Maximum participation to preferred:
4,000 x $100 x 5% = $20,000

Allocation based on outstanding
stock at total par value (preferred
cannot receive more than $20,000)

Total par value
of preferred:        $400,000      76.92%
Total par value
of common:            120,000      23.08%
                     $520,000     100.00%

Remaining dividend to allocate:
($50,000 - $32,000 - $9,600) = $8,400

Preferred: 76.92% x $8,400        6,461
Common:    23.08% x $8,400

|  | Preferred | Common |
|---|---|---|
|  |  | 1,939 |
|  | $38,461 | $11,539 |

d.  Year 1
    Preferred
    4,000 x $100 x 8% = $32,000
    The entire $25,000 in year 1
    goes to preferred.

    Year 2
    Preferred
    4,000 x $100 x 8% = $32,000
    The remaining dividend go
    to common ($50,000-$32,000).

| | Preferred | Common |
|---|---|---|
| Year 1 | $25,000 | -0- |
| Year 2 | $32,000 | $18,000 |
| | $32,000 | $18,000 |

# Chapter 4: Income Statement

<u>Chapter 4 - Problem 1 - Supply the Words Necessary to Complete
the Following Items</u>

1.  The income statement is often considered to be the most
    _____ financial statement.

2.  An income statement summarizes revenues and expenses and
    gains and losses, and ends with the ___ _____ for a specific
    _____.

3.  Cost of goods sold shows the cost of goods sold to produce
    _____.

4.  Unusual or infrequent items are either _____ or _____
    infrequently.

5.  Equity earnings (losses) are the investor's _____ share
    of the _____ earnings (losses).

6.  To the extent that equity earnings are not accompanied by
    _____ dividends, the investor reports earnings greater than
    the _____ flow from the investments.

7.  Extraordinary items are material events and transactions
    distinguished by their _____ nature and by the _____ of
    their occurrence.

8.  The cumulative effect of a change in accounting principle
    should be removed from the income statement for _____
    analysis.

9.  If a firm consolidates subsidiaries not wholly owned, the
    _____ revenues and expenses of the subsidiaries are included
    with those of the _____.

10. The reconciliation of retained earnings usually appears as part of a statement of _____ equity.

11. A cash dividend declared by the board of directors reduces _____ _____ by the amount of the dividends declared and creates the current liability, _____ _____.

12. A stock dividend should reduce the _____ value of individual shares by the _____ of the stock dividend.

13. A stock split merely _____ the number of shares of stock.

14. The legality of distributions to stockholders is governed by _____ law.

15. Comprehensive income will typically be more _____ than net income.


## Chapter 4 - Problem 2 - Multiple Choice

Choose the best answer for each of the following questions and enter the identifying letter in the space provided.

_____ 1. Which of the following items would be classified as operating revenue or expense on an income statement of a manufacturing firm?

     a. interest expense
     b. advertising expense
     c. equity income
     d. dividend income
     e. cumulative effect of change in accounting principle

_____ 2. Which of the following is a recurring item?

     a. error of a prior period
     b. equity in earnings of nonconsolidated subsidiaries
     c. extraordinary loss
     d. cumulative effect of change in accounting principle
     e. discontinued operations

_____ 3. The following relate to the income statement of Growth Company for the year ended 19X9. What is the beginning inventory?

| | |
|---|---|
| Purchases | $180,000 |
| Purchase returns | 5,000 |
| Sales | 240,000 |
| Cost of goods sold | 210,000 |
| Ending inventory | 30,000 |

    a. $ 6,000
    b. $65,000
    c. $50,000
    d. $55,000
    e. $70,000

_____ 4. Which of the following items are **not** considered to be nonrecurring items?

    a. unusual or infrequent item disclosed separately
    b. discontinued operations
    c. extraordinary item
    d. cumulative effect of change in accounting principle
    e. all of the above

_____ 5. If the investor company owns 30% of the stock of the investee company and the investee company reports profits of $150,000, then the investor company reports equity income of:

    a. $25,000
    b. $35,000
    c. $45,000
    d. $50,000
    e. $55,000

_____ 6. Which of the following items on the income statement is not disclosed net of tax?

    a. unusual or infrequent item disclosed separately
    b. discontinued operations
    c. extraordinary loss
    d. cumulative effect of change in accounting principle
    e. items (b) and (c) are both not disclosed net of tax

_____ 7. Which of the following would be classified as an extraordinary item on the income statement?

    a. loss from tornado
    b. loss on disposal of a segment of business
    c. write-down of inventory
    d. correction of an error of the current period
    e. loss from strike

_____ 8. In the general case when a change in accounting principle is made, special disclosure is required that includes the following:

    a. show as an extraordinary item.
    b. show as an unusual or infrequent item.
    c. make a retroactive adjustment for prior years.
    d. disclose the cumulative effect of the change upon prior periods' income in the income for the period of the change.
    e. do not change the income statement in the period of change.

_____ 9. The statement of retained earnings will disclose:

    a. disposal of a segment of the business.
    b. cumulative effect of a change in accounting principle.
    c. extraordinary items.
    d. adjustments of errors of prior years.
    e. adjustments of errors of the current year.

_____ 10. Which of the following is true when a cash dividend is declared and paid?

    a. The firm is left with a liability to pay the dividend.
    b. Retained earnings is reduced by the amount of the dividend.
    c. Retained earnings is increased by the amount of the dividend.
    d. Retained earnings is not influenced by the dividend.
    e. Stockholders' equity is increased.

_____ 11.  Which of the following is true when a 10% stock dividend is declared and distributed?

    a.  Retained earnings is increased.
    b.  Stockholders' equity is increased.
    c.  Stockholders' equity is decreased.
    d.  Authorized shares are increased.
    e.  The overall effect is to leave stockholders' equity in total and each owner's share of stockholders' equity unchanged; however, the total number of shares increase.

_____ 12.  The following relate to Owens Data in 19XX.  What is the ending inventory?

| | |
|---|---|
| Purchases | $580,000 |
| Beginning inventory | 80,000 |
| Purchase returns | 8,000 |
| Sales | 900,000 |
| Cost of goods sold | 520,000 |

    a.  $150,000
    b.  $132,000
    c.  $152,000
    d.  $170,000
    e.  $142,000

_____ 13.  Changes in account balances of Gross Flowers during 19XX were:

| | Increase |
|---|---|
| Assets | $400,000 |
| Liabilities | 150,000 |
| Capital stock | 120,000 |
| Additional paid-in capital | 110,000 |

Assuming there were no charges to retained earnings other than dividends of $20,000, the net income (loss) for 19XX was:

    a.  ($20,000)
    b.  ($40,000)
    c.  $20,000
    d.  $40,000
    e.  $60,000

_____ 14. Which of the following would be classified as an extraordinary item on the income statement?

    a.  loss on disposal of a segment of business
    b.  cumulative effect of a change in accounting principle
    c.  a sale of fixed assets
    d.  an error correction that relates to a prior year
    e.  a loss from a flood in a location that would not be expected to flood

_____ 15. Minority share of earnings comes from the following situation:

    a.  A company has been consolidated with our income statement and our company owns less than 100% of the other company.
    b.  A company has been consolidated with our income statement and our company owns 100% of the other company.
    c.  Our company owns less than 100% of another company and the statements are not consolidated.
    d.  Our company owns 100% of another company and the statements are not consolidated.
    e.  none of the above.

_____ 16. Which of the following will **not** be disclosed in retained earnings?

    a.  declaration of a stock dividend
    b.  adjustment for an error of the current period
    c.  adjustment for an error of a prior period
    d.  net income
    e.  net loss

_____ 17. Bell Company has 2,000,000 shares of common stock with par of $10. Additional paid-in capital totals $15,000,000 and retained earnings is $15,000,000. The Directors declare a 5% stock dividend when the market value is $10. The reduction of retained earnings as a result of the declaration will be:

    a.  $0
    b.  $1,000,000
    c.  $800,000
    d.  $600,000
    e.  none of the above

_____ 18. The stockholders' equity of Gaffney Company at November 30, 2002, is presented below:

Common stock, par value $5,
  authorized 200,000 shares,
    100,000 shares issued and outstanding   $500,000
Paid-in-capital in excess of par          100,000
Retained earnings                    300,000
                                  $900,000

On December 1, 2002, the Board of Directors of Gaffney Company declared a 5% stock dividend, to be distributed on December 20th. The market price of the common on December 1 was $10, and $12 on December 20th. What is the amount of the charge to retained earnings as a result of the declaration and distribution of this stock dividend?

a. $0
b. $40,000
c. $50,000
d. $60,000
e. none of the above

_____ 19. Schroeder Company had 200,000 shares of common stock outstanding with a $2 par value and retained earnings of $90,000. In 2001, earnings per share were $.50. In 2002, they split the stock 2 for 1. Which of the following would result from the stock split?

a. Retained earnings will decrease as a result of the stock split.
b. 400,000 shares of common stock will be outstanding.
c. The par value would become $4 par.
d. Retained earnings will increase as a result of the stock split.
e. None of the above.

_____ 20. Which of the following is <u>not</u> a category within accumulated other comprehensive income?

a. Foreign currency translation adjustments
b. Unrealized holding gains and losses on available-for-sale marketable securities
c. Changes to stockholders' equity resulting from additional minimum pension liability.
d. Unrealized gains and losses from derivative instruments
e. Extraordinary item

Chapter 4 - Problem 3 - True/False

Indicate whether each of the following is true (T) or false (F) in the space provided.

_____ 1. Consolidated statements reflect an economic, rather than a legal, concept of entity.

_____ 2. Where the operations of the parent and subsidiary are not complementary, then these firms are not consolidated even if control is present.

_____ 3. Most firms surveyed use some type of single-step format for the income statement.

_____ 4. Income from operations would usually be more than gross profit.

_____ 5. An unusual or infrequent item should be disclosed on the income statement, net of tax.

_____ 6. If an investor company reports material equity earnings, then its ability to pay cash dividends may be much less than indicated by the reported net income.

_____ 7. A separate income statement category for the gain or loss from disposal of a segment of a business must be presented net of tax.

_____ 8. In analysis of income for purposes of determining a trend, extraordinary items should be eliminated.

_____ 9. In the general case, generally accepted accounting principles require retroactive adjustments when applying a new accounting principle.

_____ 10. If a firm consolidates subsidiaries that are not wholly owned, then usually a proportionate amount of revenues and expenses of the subsidiaries are included with those of the parent.

_____ 11. An income statement summarizes revenues and expenses and gains and losses, and ends with the net income for a specific period.

_____ 12. The statement of retained earnings summarizes the changes to retained earnings.

_____ 13. A common device to increase stockholders' equity is a stock split.

_____ 14. Interim reports focus primarily on the income statement.

_____ 15. The income statement is frequently considered to be the most important financial statement.

_____ 16. Gross profit is usually a prominent figure on a multiple-step income statement.

_____ 17. "Other income" and "other expense" relate directly to the operations of the firm.

_____ 18. Equity earnings can be more or less than the cash flow from the related investment.

_____ 19. Ideally, net income is the better income figure to use to project the future from the analysis of historical statements.

_____ 20. Since the number of shares changes under both a stock dividend and a stock split, any ratio based on the number of shares must be restated.

_____ 21. The legality of distributions to stockholders is governed by applicable state law.

_____ 22. The accounting standard provides considerable flexibility in reporting comprehensive income.

# Chapter 4 - Problem 4 - Matching Terms

Listed below are several terms. Match the letter that goes with each description.

a. stock dividend
b. cash dividend
c. stock split
d. extraordinary items
e. discontinued operations
f. equity in earnings of nonconsolidated subsidiaries
g. unusual or infrequent item
h. cumulative effect of change in accounting principle
i. minority share of earnings
j. retained earnings

_____ 1. Certain income statement items that are unusual or occur infrequently, but not both.

_____ 2. Material events and transactions distinguished by their unusual nature and infrequent occurrence.

_____ 3. A dividend in the form of additional shares of a company's stock.

_____ 4. Increase in the number of shares of a class of capital stock, with no change in the total dollar amount of the class, but with a converse reduction in the par or stated value of the shares.

_____ 5. When a firm has investments in stocks, uses the equity method of accounting, and the investment is not consolidated.

_____ 6. The payment (receipt) of a dividend in cash.

_____ 7. The disposal of a major segment of a business.

_____ 8. Undistributed earnings of the corporation.

_____ 9. The portion of income that belongs to the minority owners of a firm that has been consolidated.

_____ 10. The effect that a new accounting principle would have had on net income of prior periods if it had been used instead of the old principle.

# Chapter 4 - Problem 5 - Income Statement Classification

Indicate the section of a multiple-step income statement in which each of the following items would usually appear. Use Exhibit 4-3 in the book as a guide. If the item would not be present on the income statement, use an "N".

_____  1.  depreciation for salesperson's car

_____  2.  factory supplies used

_____  3.  electricity expense related to the factory

_____  4.  tornado loss, net of tax

_____  5.  rent income for a manufacturing company

_____  6.  dividends paid

_____  7.  gain related to prior years that results from a change in accounting principle

_____  8.  dividend income

# Chapter 4 - Problem 6 - Multiple-Step Income Statement

The following information for Thacker Company covers the year ended 2001:

| | |
|---|---:|
| Dividend income | $ 5,000 |
| Dividend paid | 10,000 |
| Selling expenses | 15,000 |
| Administrative expenses | 18,000 |
| Sales | 200,000 |
| Purchases | 80,000 |
| Extraordinary loss (net of tax) | 10,000 |
| Merchandise inventory, 1/1 | 120,000 |
| Merchandise inventory, 12/31 | 130,000 |
| Interest expense | 10,000 |
| Interest income | 8,000 |
| Income taxes | 40,000 |
| Retained earnings | 120,000 |

**Required:** a. Prepare a multiple-step income statement.

b. Prepare a single-step income statement. (Present income taxes with expenses.)

# Chapter 4 - Problem 7 - Determine the Financial Statement

List the statement on which each of these may appear.  Choose
from (1) income statement, (2) balance sheet, or (3) statement of
retained earnings.

|        |    |                                                   |
|--------|----|---------------------------------------------------|
| _____ | a. | sales                                             |
| _____ | b. | taxes payable                                     |
| _____ | c. | accounts receivable                               |
| _____ | d. | accumulated deprecation                           |
| _____ | e. | dividends paid                                    |
| _____ | f. | minority share of earnings                        |
| _____ | g. | cumulative effect of change in accounting principle |
| _____ | h. | depreciation expense                              |
| _____ | i. | common stock outstanding                          |
| _____ | j. | accounts payable                                  |
| _____ | k. | cost of goods sold                                |
| _____ | l. | adjustments of prior periods                      |
| _____ | m. | land                                              |
| _____ | n. | notes payable                                     |
| _____ | o. | treasury stock                                    |

# Chapter 4 - Problem 8 - Equity Earnings

Graham Company owns 30% of Cooper Company and accounts for the
investment on the equity basis and does not consolidate.  At the
beginning of 2001, the investment in Cooper Company was $200,000.
In 2001, Cooper Company earned $50,000 and paid dividends of
$5,000.

**Required:**  
a. What amount will Graham Company report as equity
   income in earnings of Cooper Company in 2001?

b. What amount of cash flow will Graham Company
   receive from Cooper Company in 2001?

c. Why does recognition of equity earnings cause
   problems in analysis?

## Chapter 4 - Problem 9 - Minority Interest

Zero Inc. owns 80% of Jammit Inc. and consolidates this
subsidiary.  In 2001, Jammit Inc. earned $60,000 after tax and
Zero Inc. earned $500,000.  The total stockholders' equity of
Jammit Inc. at the end of 2001 was $700,000.

**Required:**
    a.    Determine the minority share of earnings reported
        by Zero Inc. for 2001.
    b.    Determine the consolidated net income of Zero Inc.
    c.    Determine the minority interest at the end of 2001
        on the balance sheet of Zero Inc.
    d.    How should minority interest be classified on the
        balance sheet for analysis?

Chapter 4 - Problem 10 - Retained Earnings

The following information is available for Toledo Company at the
end of 2002:

| | |
|---|---:|
| Current assets | $200,000 |
| Property, plant, and equipment, net | 500,000 |
| Investments | 100,000 |
| Current liabilities | 150,000 |
| Long-term liabilities | 400,000 |
| Income for 2002 | 50,000 |
| Common stock | 100,000 |
| Dividends declared and paid during 2002 | 20,000 |

**Required:**   a.   Determine the balance in retained earnings at the
end of 2002.

               b.   Determine the balance in retained earnings at the
end of 2001.

# Chapter 4 - Problem 11 - Nonrecurring Items

The income statement of Rocket Company for the year ended December 31, 2002, shows:

| | |
|---|---:|
| Sales | $900,000 |
| Cost of goods sold | 500,000 |
| Gross profit | 400,000 |
| Operating expenses | (100,000) |
| Equity earnings of nonconsolidated subsidiaries | 20,000 |
| Operating income before income taxes | 320,000 |
| Taxes related to operations | (100,000) |
| Net income from operations before cumulative effect of change in accounting principle | 220,000 |
| Cumulative effect of change in accounting principle (less applicable income taxes of $20,000) | 50,000 |
| Net income | $270,000 |

**Required:**  a.  Compute the net earnings after removing nonrecurring items.

             b.  Determine the earnings from the nonconsolidated subsidiary.

             c.  Determine the total tax amount.

## CHAPTER 4 - SOLUTIONS

Chapter 4 - Problem 1 - Supply the Words Necessary to Complete the Following Items

1. important

2. net income; period

3. revenue

4. unusual; occur

5. proportionate; investee's

6. cash; cash

7. unusual; infrequency

8. primary

9. total; parent

10. stockholders

11. retained earnings; dividends payable

12. market; percentage

13. increases

14. state

15. volatile

# Chapter 4 - Problem 2 - Multiple Choice

__b__   1.  Advertising expense would be classified as operating expense of a manufacturing firm.

__b__   2.  Equity in earnings of nonconsolidated subsidiaries would be considered to be a recurring item.

__b__   3.

| | | |
|---|---|---|
| Beginning inventory | | $ 65,000 Computed |
| Purchases | $180,000 | |
| Purchases returns | (5,000) | 175,000 |
| Total available | | 240,000 Computed |
| Less ending inventory | | (30,000) |
| Cost of goods sold | | $210,000 |

__a.__   4.  Unusual or infrequent items disclosed separately are reported with normal, recurring revenues, expenses, gains, and losses.

__c__   5.  30% x $150,000 = $45,000

__a__   6.  Unusual or infrequent items are disclosed separately, before tax.

__a__   7.  Extraordinary items are material events and transactions distinguished by their unusual nature and by the infrequency of their occurrence. A loss from a tornado would qualify as an extraordinary item.

__d__   8.  The reporting guideline directs that the income effect of the change on prior years be reported net of tax as a cumulative effect of change in accounting principle on the income statement in the year of change.

__d__   9.  Adjustments of errors of prior years are handled as prior period adjustments.

__b__  10.  A cash dividend declared by the board of directors reduces retained earnings by the amount of the dividend declared.

__e__  11.  The overall effect of a stock dividend leaves total stockholders' equity and each owner's share of stockholders' equity unchanged. However, the total number of outstanding shares increases.

b    12.    Beginning inventory          $  80,000
            Purchases                    $580,000
            Purchase returns             (  8,000)
            Total available               652,000
            Less ending inventory        (132,000)
            Cost of goods sold           $520,000

d    13.    Assets Increase              $400,000
            The increase in assets is equal to the
            change in liabilities and stockholders' equity.

            Liabilities increase                    $150,000
            Capital stock increases                  120,000
            Additional paid-in capital increases     110,000
                                                    $380,000
            Therefore, increase to retained earnings  20,000
                                                    $400,000

            Decrease to retained earnings
              related to dividends       $<20,000>
            Net increase to retained earnings       $ 20,000
            Therefore, net income was    $ 40,000

e    14.    An extraordinary item is a material event
            or transaction distinguished by unusual
            nature and by infrequency of occurrence.

a    15.    If a firm consolidates subsidiaries not
            wholly owned, the total revenues and expenses
            of the subsidiaries are included with those of
            the parent.  However, to determine the income
            that would accrue to the parent, it is
            necessary to deduct the portion of income
            that would belong to the minority owners.

b    16.    An adjustment for an error of the current period is
            adjusted during the current period.

b    17.    2,000,000 x .5% = 100,000 x $10 = $1,000,000

c    18.    100,000 x .5% = 5,000 x $10 = $50,000

b    19.    200,000 x 2 = 400,000

e    20.    Extraordinary items are not part of accumulated other
            comprehensive income.

Chapter 4 - Problem 3 - True/False

| | | | | | | | | | | |
|---|---|---|---|---|---|---|---|---|---|---|
| T | 1. | T | 6. | T | 11. | T | 16. | T | 21. |
| F | 2. | T | 7. | T | 12. | F | 17. | T | 22. |
| T | 3. | T | 8. | F | 13. | T | 18. | | |
| F | 4. | F | 9. | T | 14. | F | 19. | | |
| F | 5. | F | 10. | T | 15. | T | 20. | | |


Chapter 4 - Problem 4 - Matching Terms

| | | | |
|---|---|---|---|
| g | 1. | b | 6. |
| d | 2. | e | 7. |
| a | 3. | j | 8. |
| c | 4. | i | 9. |
| f | 5. | h | 10. |


Chapter 4 - Problem 5 - Income Statement Classification

1.    operating expenses
2.    cost of products sold
3.    cost of products sold
4.    extraordinary loss
5.    other income
6.    "N"
7.    cumulative effect of change in accounting principle
8.    other income

# Chapter 4 - Problem 6 - Multiple-Step Income Statement

a.   Multiple-step income statement:

**Thacker Company**
**Income Statement**
**For the Year Ended December 31, 2001**

| | | |
|---|---:|---:|
| Sales | | $200,000 |
| Cost of sales: | | |
| Beginning inventory | $120,000 | |
| Purchases | 80,000 | |
| Merchandise available for sale | 200,000 | |
| Less: Ending inventory | (130,000) | |
| Cost of sales | | (70,000) |
| Gross profit | | 130,000 |
| Operating expense: | | |
| Selling expense | $ 15,000 | |
| Administrative expenses | 18,000 | (33,000) |
| Operating income | | 97,000 |
| Other income: | | |
| Dividend income | $  5,000 | |
| Interest income | 8,000 | 13,000 |
| | | 110,000 |
| Other expense: | | |
| Interest expense | | (10,000) |
| Income before taxes and | | |
|   extraordinary loss | | 100,000 |
| Income taxes | | (40,000) |
| Income before extraordinary loss | | 60,000 |
| Extraordinary loss, net of tax | | (10,000) |
| Net income | | $ 50,000 |

b.    Single-step income statement:

Thacker Company
Income Statement
For the Year Ended December 31, 2001

| | | |
|---|---|---|
| Revenue: | | |
| Sales | | $200,000 |
| Other income: | | |
| Interest income | $8,000 | |
| Dividend income | 5,000 | 13,000 |
| Total revenue | | 213,000 |
| | | |
| Expenses: | | |
| Cost of sales | | (70,000) |
| Administrative expenses | | (18,000) |
| Selling expenses | | (15,000) |
| Interest expense | | (10,000) |
| Income taxes | | (40,000) |
| Total expenses | | 153,000 |
| | | |
| Income before extraordinary loss | | 60,000 |
| Extraordinary loss, net of tax | | (10,000) |
| Net income | | $ 50,000 |

Chapter 4 - Problem 7 - Determine the Financial Statement

| | |
|---|---|
| 1 | a. |
| 2 | b. |
| 2 | c. |
| 2 | d. |
| 3 | e. |
| 1 | f. |
| 1 | g. |
| 1 | h. |
| 2 | i. |
| 2 | j. |
| 1 | k. |
| 3 | l. |
| 2 | m. |
| 2 | n. |
| 2 | o. |

Chapter 4 - Problem 8 - Equity Earnings

a.    $50,000 x 30% = $15,000

b.    $5,000 x 30% = $1,500

c.    Equity earnings cause a problem in analysis because the
      amount of earnings are usually different than the cash
      generated, as was illustrated in (a) and (b). Equity
      earnings also relate to profits of another company.

Chapter 4 - Problem 9 - Minority Interest

a.    20% x $60,000 = $12,000

b.    $500,000    Zero Inc.
        60,000    Jammit Inc.
       (12,000)    20% x $60,000 = $12,000
      $548,000

c.    $700,000 x 20% = $140,000

d.    Minority interest is best classified as a liability.

Chapter 4 - Problem 10 - Retained Earnings

a.
| Current assets | $200,000 | Current liabilities | $150,000 |
|---|---|---|---|
| Property, plant, | | Long-term liabilities | 400,000 |
|   and equipment, | | Common stock | 100,000 |
|   net | 500,000 | Retained earnings | ? |
| Investments | 100,000 | Total | $800,000 |
| Total | $800,000 | | |

      The retained earnings was $150,000

b.    Retained earnings, December 31, 2002            $150,000
      + Dividends                                       20,000
                                                       170,000
      - Net income                                     (50,000)
      Retained earnings, December 31, 2001            $120,000

Chapter 4 - Problem 11 - Nonrecurring Items

a.    $270,000
       (50,000)
      $220,000

b.    $20,000

c.    $100,000
        20,000
      $120,000

# Chapter 5: Basics of Analysis

<u>Chapter 5 - Problem 1 - Supply the Words Necessary to Complete
the Following Items</u>

1. Comparison of income statement and balance sheet numbers, in
   the form of _____, can create difficulties due to the
   _____ of the financial statements.

2. In _____ _____, a figure from a year is compared
   with a base selected from the _____ _____.

3. In _____ _____, a dollar figure for an account
   is expressed in terms of that same account figure for a
   selected _____ _____.

4. Using the past history of a firm for comparison is called
   _____ _____.

5. The analysis of an entity's financial statements can be more
   meaningful if the results are compared with _____
   _____ and with results of _____.

6. The <u>Department of Commerce Financial Report</u> is a publication
   of the _____ _____ for manufacturing, mining, and
   trade corporations.

7. A particular advantage of Robert Morris Associates <u>Annual
   Statement Studies</u> is that this source provides simple,
   common-size _____ _____ and _____ _____ as
   well as _____ selected items.

8. The <u>Standard and Poor's Industry Surveys</u> contains a _____
   _____ summary on several firms within an _____ group.

9. The <u>Almanac of Business and Industrial Financial Ratios</u>
   presents _____ statistics for _____ _____ categories of
   firms.

10. The <u>Value Line Investment Service</u> rates 1,700 firms stock
    for _____ and _____.

11. Financial statement analysis is an _____; it requires judgment decisions on the part of the _____.

12. The standard _____ _____ was developed for use in the classification of establishments by _____ of activity in which they are engaged.

13. Comparisons of firms of different _____ may be more difficult than comparison of firms of equal _____.

14. The components of financial statements will vary by _____ of industry.

15. There is a difference between the objectives that are sought by _____-_____ grantors of credit and those sought by _____-_____ grantors of credit.


## Chapter 5 - Problem 2 - Multiple Choice

Choose the best answer for each of the following questions and enter the identifying letter in the spaces provided.

_____ 1. Which of the following statements is **incorrect**?

   a. Ratios are fractions expressed in percent or times per year.
   b. A ratio can be computed from any pair of numbers.
   c. A very long list of meaningful ratios can be derived.
   d. There is no standard list of ratios.
   e. Comparison of income statement and balance sheet numbers, in the form of ratios, should not be done.

_____ 2. Comparing a figure from this year's statement with a base selected from the current year results in a(n):

   a. vertical common-size statement
   b. horizontal common-size statement
   c. funds statement
   d. absolute figure
   e. balance sheet

_____ 3. Fremont Electronics has income of $1,000,000.
Columbus Electronics has income of $2,000,000. Which
of the following statements is a **correct** statement?

   a. Columbus Electronics is getting a higher return on
      assets employed.
   b. Columbus Electronics has higher profit margins
      than does Fremont Electronics.
   c. Fremont Electronics could be more profitable than
      Columbus Electronics in relation to resources
      employed.
   d. No comparison can be made between Fremont
      Electronics and Columbus Electronics.
   e. Fremont Electronics is not making good use of its
      resources.

_____ 4. A financial service that provides common-size income
statements and balance sheets as well as sixteen
selected ratios:

   a. Dun's Business Month
   b. Standard and Poor's Industry Surveys
   c. Robert Morris Associates Annual Statement Studies
   d. The Almanac of Business and Industrial Financial
      Ratios
   e. The FTC Quarterly Financial Report

_____ 5. Industry ratios should **not** be considered as absolute
norms for a given industry because of all but one of
the following:

   a. the firms have different accounting methods
   b. many companies have varied product lines
   c. companies within the same industry may differ in
      their method of operations
   d. the fiscal year-ends of the companies may differ
   e. the financial services may be private independent
      firms

_____ 6. A publication of the federal government for manufacturing, mining, and trade corporations.

    a. Robert Morris Associates Annual Statement Studies
    b. Standard and Poor's Industry Surveys
    c. The Almanac of Business and Industrial Financial Ratios
    d. Dun's
    e. The FTC Quarterly Financial Report

_____ 7. This service represents a compilation of corporate tax return data.

    a. Robert Morris Associates Annual Statement Studies
    b. Standard and Poor's Industry Surveys
    c. The Almanac of Business and Industrial Financial Ratios
    d. Dun's
    e. The FTC Quarterly Financial Report

_____ 8. This service includes over 800 different lines of business.

    a. Robert Morris Associates Annual Statement Studies
    b. Standard and Poor's Industry Surveys
    c. The Almanac of Business Industry Surveys
    d. Industry Norms and Key Business Ratios, desk-top edition
    e. The FTC Quarterly Financial Report

_____ 9. Robert Morris Associates Annual Statement Studies reported the following figures for manufacturers of pressed and blown glass and glassware for a ratio: 10.8, 3.4, and 2.4. Which of the following is correct?

    a. one third of each of the companies experienced each of the amounts
    b. the best firm had 10.8
    c. the worst firm had 2.4
    d. the median was 3.4; 10.8 is the figure for the upper quartile; 2.4 is the figure for the lower quartile
    e. none of the above is correct

_____ 10. A manufacturing firm will usually have large inventories composed of:

a. raw materials
b. work in process
c. finished goods
d. a, b, and c
e. b and c only

_____ 11. This analysis compares each amount with a base amount for a selected base year.

a. vertical common-size
b. horizontal common-size
c. funds statement
d. common-size statement
e. none of these

_____ 12. Howell Electro has net income of $1,000,000. Franks Electro has net income of $1,250,000. Which of the following best compares the profitability of Howell and Franks?

a. Franks Electro is 25% more profitable than Howell Electro.
b. Franks Electro is less profitable than Howell Electro.
c. Franks Electro is more profitable than Howell Electric.
d. More information is needed, such as relative size of the firms, to draw reasonable conclusions on profitability.
e. Howell Electro is 30% more profitable than Franks Electro.

_____ 13. Suppose you are comparing two firms in the coal industry. Which type of numbers would be most meaningful for statement analysis?

    a. Relative numbers would be most meaningful for both firms, especially for interfirm comparisons.
    b. Relative numbers are not meaningful.
    c. Absolute numbers would be most meaningful.
    d. Absolute numbers are not relevant.
    e. It is not meaningful to compare two firms.

_____ 14. This service contains profitability and investment data for 1,700 individual firms and for industries in general. This service rates each stock's timeliness and safety.

    a. Standard and Poor's Industry Surveys
    b. Value Line Investment Service
    c. Department of Commerce Financial Report
    d. Robert Morris Associates Annual Statement Studies
    e. The Almanac of Business and Industrial Financial Ratios

_____ 15. Management is a user of financial analysis. Which of the following comments does not represent a fair statement as to the management perspective?

    a. Management is not interested in the view of investors.
    b. Management is interested in liquidity.
    c. Management is interested in profitability.
    d. Management is interested in the debt position.
    e. Management is interested in the financial structure of the entity.

Chapter 5 - Problem 3 - True/False

Indicate whether each of the following is true (T) or false (F) in the space provided.

_____  1.  Ratios are fractions expressed in percent or times.

_____  2.  For meaningful ratios analysis a standard list of ratios should be computed regardless of the objective of the analysis.

_____  3.  Comparison of income statement and balance sheet numbers, in the form of ratios, can create difficulties due to the timing of the financial statements.

_____  4.  The use of absolute figures is usually preferable to the use of percent when performing analysis.

_____  5.  Care must be exercised in the use of common size analysis when the absolute figures are small.

_____  6.  In horizontal analysis, a figure from this year's statement is compared with a comparable item in the base year.

_____  7.  Comparisons are helpful in making ratios more meaningful for a given firm.

_____  8.  By looking at a particular ratio one can draw definite conclusions as to the liquidity of a firm.

_____  9.  Both the analyst and the financial services are faced with the problem of determining the industry that the company best fits.

_____  10.  "The Ratios" published by Dun and Bradstreet include a median figure, an upper quartile figure, and a lower quartile figure for each ratio included.

_____  11.  Industry averages should be regarded as general guidelines and not as absolute industry norms.

_____  12.  The financial position or structure of a small firm is often quite similar to that of a large firm.

_____  13.  The industry ratio formulas often vary from source to source.

_____ 14. Cost of goods sold will often represent the major expense for a manufacturing firm.

_____ 15. There is no major difference between the objectives that are sought by short-time grantors of credit and those sought by long-term grantors of credit.

_____ 16. A given ratio is always computed the same way, regardless of the source.

_____ 17. The year end will have an impact on ratio results.

# CHAPTER 5 - SOLUTIONS

## Chapter 5 - Problem 1 - Supply the Words Necessary to Complete The Following Items

1. ratios; timing

2. vertical analysis; same year

3. horizontal analysis; base year

4. trend analysis

5. industry averages; competitors

6. federal government

7. income statements; balance sheets; sixteen

8. five-year; industry

9. fifty; eleven size

10. timeliness; safety

11. art; analyst

12. industrial classification; type

13. size; size

14. type

15. short-term; long-term

## Chapter 5 - Problem 2 - Multiple Choice

__e__ 1. Most ratios are computed comparing selected income statement and balance sheet numbers.

__a__ 2. A figure from this year's statement is compared with a base selected from the current year. This would be described as a vertical common-size statement.

__c__ 3. Since we do not know the resources employed, Fremont Electronics could be more profitable than Columbus Electronics in relation to resources employed.

__c__ 4. Robert Morris Associates Annual Statement Studies provides common-size income statements and balance sheets as well as sixteen selected ratios.

e    5. The fact that financial services may be private independent firms does not relate to industry ratios being considered as absolute norms for a given industry.

e    6. The FTC Quarterly Financial Report is a publication of the federal government for manufacturing, mining, and trade corporations.

c    7. The Almanac of Business and Industrial Financial Ratios, by Leo Troy, represents a compilation of corporate tax return data.

d    8. Industry Norms and Key Business Ratios, desk-top edition, included 800 different lines of business.

d    9. The high number represents the figure for the upper quartile, the center number represents the median, and the low number represents the lower quartile.

d   10. A manufacturing firm will usually have large inventories composed of raw materials, work in process, and finished goods.

b   11. A horizontal analysis compares each amount with a base amount for a selected base year.

d   12. More information is needed to compare the profitability of Howell and Franks.

a   13. Relative numbers would be most meaningful for comparing two firms in the coal industry.

b   14. Value Line Investment Service contains profitability and investment data for 1,700 individual firms and for industries in general.

a   15. The statement "management is not interested in the view of investors" does not represent a fair statement as to the management perspective.

## Chapter 5 - Problem 3 - True/False

| | | | | | | | |
|---|---|---|---|---|---|---|---|
| T | 1. | T | 6. | T | 11. | F | 16. |
| F | 2. | T | 7. | F | 12. | T | 17. |
| T | 3. | F | 8. | T | 13. | | |
| F | 4. | T | 9. | T | 14. | | |
| T | 5. | T | 10. | F | 15. | | |

# Chapter 6: Liquidity of Short-Term Assets; Related Debt-Paying Ability

Chapter 6 - Problem 1 - Supply the Words Necessary to Complete the Following Items

1. If the entity cannot maintain a _____-\_\_\_\_\_ debt-paying ability, naturally it will not be able to maintain a \_\_\_\_\_-\_\_\_\_\_ debt-paying ability.

2. Current assets are assets that (1) are in the form of cash, (2) will be realized in cash, or (3) conserve the use of cash within the _____ _____ of a business or for \_\_\_\_ \_\_\_\_\_, whichever is _____.

3. There are five categories of assets that are usually found in current assets: cash, _____ _____, _____, _____, and prepayments.

4. The _____ _____ represents the period of time elapsing between the acquisition of goods and the final _____ realization resulting from sales and subsequent collections.

5. Cash is a medium of exchange that a bank will _____ for deposit and a creditor will _____ for payment.

6. In order to classify cash as a current asset, it must be free from any _____ that would prevent its _____ or use to pay creditors classified as _____.

7. Compensating balances reduce the amount of cash available to the borrower to meet _____, and they increase the _____ _____ rate.

8. Two major problems encountered when analyzing a current asset are the problems of determining a fair _____ for the asset and the _____ of the asset.

9. To qualify as a marketable security, the investment must be readily _____ and it must be the intent of management to convert the investment to _____ within the current _____ _____ or one year, whichever is _____.

10. In terms of liquidity, it is to management's _____ to show investments under _____ _____, instead of long-term investments, because this classification improves the _____ appearance of the firm.

11. When it is detected that the same securities are carried as marketable securities year after year, to be _____, it is better to reclassify these securities as _____ for analysis purposes.

12. Investments classified as marketable securities should be _____.

13. The valuation problem from waiting to collect is ignored in the _____ of receivables and of notes that are classified in _____ _____.

14. For receivables, the direct write-off method frequently results in the bad debt _____ being recognized in the _____ subsequent to the sale and thus does not result in a proper _____ of expense with revenue.

15. Claims from customers are usually in the form of _____ _____.

16. Usually, a note is for a _____ period of time than an account receivable and is _____-_____.

17. Under the condition that the face amount of the note does not represent the _____ _____ of the consideration exchanged, the note is recorded as a _____ _____ amount on the date of the original transaction.

18. The use of the allowance for doubtful accounts approach results in the bad debt expense being charged to the _____ ___ _____.

19. When a company has receivables classified as current, based on _____ _____, special note should be made of this when comparing with _____.

20. Customer concentration can be an important consideration in the _____ of receivables.

21. Two problems exist in the valuation of a receivable: one is that a period of time must pass before the receivable can be _____, and the other problem is that collection may _____ be made.

22. The number of days' sales in receivables relates the amount of the _____ _____ to the average daily _____ on account.

23. For internal analysis, days' sales in receivables should be compared with the company's _____ _____ to obtain an indication of how efficiently the company is managing its _____.

24. The days' sales in receivables ratio gives an indication of the length of time that the receivables have been outstanding at the end of the year. The indication can be misleading if sales are _____ and/or the company uses a _____ _____ year.

25. In order to have a realistic indication of the liquidity of receivables, only the _____ sales should be included in the computations. If cash sales are included, the - _____ will be overstated.

26. _____ is usually the most significant asset in determining the _____-_____ debt-paying ability of an entity.

27. The basic approach to the valuation of inventory is to use _____.

28. To be classified as inventory, the asset should be held for _____ in the ordinary course of business or _____ or _____ in the production of goods.

29. A firm that purchases merchandise in a form to sell to customers is called a _____ concern. A firm that produces goods to be sold is called a _____ concern.

30. The typical cost flow assumptions for inventory are _____-___, _____-____; _____-____, _____-____; or some average computation.

31. An average cost computation for inventories results in an inventory amount and a cost of goods sold amount somewhere between the figures for _____ and _____.

32. The days' sales in inventory is an estimate of the number of _____ that it will take to _____ the current inventory.

33. Computing the average inventory based on beginning-of-year and end-of-year inventories can be _____ if the company has seasonal fluctuations or if the company uses a _____ _____ year.

34. The accounts receivable turnover in days, plus the _____ turnover in days, gives an approximation of the _____ _____.

35. Prepayments consist of unexpired _____, for which payment has been made, which are expected to be _____ within the period that has been used to determine _____ _____.

36. Current liabilities are those obligations whose _____ is reasonably expected to require the use of existing resources properly classified as _____ _____, or the creation of other current liabilities.

37. The working capital of a business is the excess of current assets over _____ _____.

38. The current ratio is determined by dividing the current assets by the _____ _____.

39. The current ratio is considered to be more indicative of short-term debt-paying ability than is the _____ _____.

40. Inventory should be removed from _____ _____ when computing the acid-test.

41. The _____ ratio indicates the immediate liquidity of the firm.

42. Relating _____ to working capital gives an indication of the turnover in working capital per year.

43. When the market value of inventory falls below ____, it is necessary to write the inventory down to the lower _____ value.

44. Following the LCM rule, inventories can be written _____ below ____ but never up above cost.

45. An opinion as to the _____ of receivables should help the analyst form an _____ of the acid-test ratio.

46. A low working capital turnover ratio tentatively indicates an _____ use of working capital.

Chapter 6 - Problem 2 - Multiple Choice

Choose the best answer for each of the following questions and enter the identifying letter in the space provided.

_____ 1. Which of the following types of businesses would probably have the longest operating cycle?

     a.  tire manufacturer
     b.  wholesale clothing store
     c.  retail clothing store
     d.  drug store
     e.  grocery store

_____ 2. Which of the following types of businesses would probably have an operating cycle that is longer than a year?

     a.  car manufacturing
     b.  winery
     c.  shoe store
     d.  bike shop
     e.  tire store

_____ 3. Abbot Company presents the following data for 2001:

| | |
|---|---:|
| Receivables, less allowance for uncollectible accounts of $16,500 | $ 325,200 |
| Net sales | 3,180,000 |
| Cost of goods sold | 3,180,000 |
| Inventory | 450,000 |

The days' sales in receivables is:

a. 54.5
b. 45.3
c. 42.5
d. 39.2
e. 35.2

_____ 4. Which of the following may be the reason that receivables appear to be low?

a. material amount of sales are on a cash basis
b. sales volume expanded materially late in the year
c. receivables have collectibility problems and possibly some should have been written off
d. the company seasonally dates invoices
e. a material amount of receivables are on the installment basis

_____ 5. Arrow Company presents the following data for 2001 and 2000:

| | 2001 | 2000 |
|---|---:|---:|
| Net sales | $3,605,600 | $3,120,500 |
| End-of-year receivables, less allowance for losses and discounts | 328,500 | 348,200 |
| Beginning-of-year receivables, less allowance for losses and discounts | 348,200 | 258,000 |

Allowance for losses and discounts:
  End of 2001 - $18,200
  End of 2000 - $15,100
  End of 1999 - $14,000

The accounts receivable turnover for 2001 and 2000 respectively is:

a. 10.16, 8.92, and appears to be improving.
b. 9.16, 9.82, and appears to be deteriorating.
c. 9.16, 10.16, and appears to be improving.
d. 8.16, 9.82, and appears to be deteriorating.
e. 10.16, 9.82, and appears to be improving.

_____ 6. Bonnet Company presents the following data for years 2001, 2000, and 1999:

|  | 2001 | 2000 | 1999 |
|---|---|---|---|
| Inventories, end of year | $ 456,500 | $ 426,500 | $ 430,000 |
| Cost of goods sold | 3,100,000 | 3,000,000 | 2,900,000 |

The days' sales in inventory for 2001 and 2000 respectively is (use ending inventory):

a. 55.50 days, 58.00 days, and appears to be improving.
b. 58.25 days, 53.75 days, and appears to be improving.
c. 53.75 days, 51.89 days, and appears to be improving.
d. 53.75 days, 51.89 days, and appears to have slightly deteriorated.
e. 51.89 days, 53.75 days, and appears to have slightly deteriorated.

_____ 7. Gonet Company presents the following data for 2001, 2000, and 1999:

|  | 2001 | 2000 | 1999 |
|---|---|---|---|
| Inventories, end of year | $ 655,000 | $ 630,000 | $580,000 |
| Cost of goods sold | 4,250,000 | 3,975,000 | 3,615,000 |

Merchandise inventory turnover for 2001 and 2000 respectively:

a. 6.07, 6.61, and appears to be improving.
b. 6.61, 6.57, and appears to be improving.
c. 6.07, 6.61, and appears to be deteriorating.
d. 6.61, 6.57, and appears to be deteriorating.
e. 6.61, 6.50, and appears to be improving.

_____ 8. Which of the following items is **not** likely to be included in current liabilities?

a. accounts payable
b. notes payable
c. preferred stock
d. accrued wages
e. collections received in advance

_____ 9. Which of the following items would **not** possibly indicate a better liquidity position than that indicated by liquidity ratios?

    a. unused bank credit lines
    b. substantial long-term assets that could be converted to cash quickly
    c. a very good long-term debt position
    d. substantial assets in investments
    e. major contingent liabilities that have not been booked

_____ 10. Company A uses lifo and Company B uses fifo for inventory valuation. Otherwise, the firms are of similar size and have the same revenue and expense. In analyzing the liquidity and profitability of the two firms, which of the following will hold true assuming inflation?

    a. Company B will normally report higher profit and lower inventory turnover.
    b. Company B will normally report lower profit and lower inventory turnover.
    c. Company A will normally report higher profit and lower inventory turnover.
    d. Company A will normally report lower profit and lower inventory turnover.
    e. It is impossible to compare two firms with different inventory methods.

_____ 11. Which of the following would best indicate that the firm is carrying excess inventory?

    a. a decline in sales
    b. an increase in sales
    c. a decline in days' sales in inventory
    d. an increasing current ratio with a declining quick ratio
    e. an increase in cost of goods sold

_____ 12. Which of the following types of businesses would normally have the shortest operating cycle?

    a. retail clothing store
    b. wholesale candy store
    c. tire manufacturers
    d. bakery selling retail only
    e. grocery store

_____ 13.  Peter Fields Company presents the following data for 2001:

Receivables, less allowance for losses
  and discounts of $10,000                    $   300,000
Net sales                                        2,800,000
Cost of goods sold                               1,900,000

The days' sales in receivables is:

a.  40.4.
b.  30.4.
c.  50.0.
d.  48.0.
e.  none of the above.

Questions 14-15 are based on the following information:

Jones Company presents the following data for 2001:

|  |  |
|---|---|
| Receivables, end of year, less allowance for losses and discounts of $120,000 | $ 2,520,000 |
| Receivables, beginning of year, less allowance for losses and discounts of $120,000 | $ 2,700,000 |
| Net sales | $26,500,000 |

_____ 14.   The accounts receivable turnover in times per year is:

    a.   10.53.
    b.    9.53.
    c.    8.53.
    d.    7.00.
    e.   none of the above.

_____ 15.   The accounts receivable turnover in days is:

    a.   35.00
    b.   40.00
    c.   37.60
    d.   75.20
    e.   none of the above

Questions 16-17 are based on the following information:

Clark Company presents the following data for 2001:

| | |
|---|---|
| Net sales, 2001 | $4,000,000 |
| Net sales, 2000 | $3,200,000 |
| Cost of goods sold, 2001 | $3,000,000 |
| Cost of goods sold, 2000 | $2,450,000 |
| Inventory, beginning of 2001 | $ 500,000 |
| Inventory, end of 2001 | $ 450,000 |

_____ 16.    The merchandise inventory turnover for 2001 is:

    a.    7.00.
    b.    7.32.
    c.    5.32.
    d.    6.32.
    e.    none of the above.

_____ 17.    The merchandise inventory turnover in days for 2001
              is:

    a.    57.79
    b.    56.00
    c.    60.00
    d.    56.79
    e.    none of the above

_____ 18. Saftner Company computed the following data for 2001:

| | |
|---|---|
| Days' sales in receivables | 36.5 days |
| Accounts receivable turnover | 9.4 times |
| Accounts receivable turnover in days | 34.4 days |
| Days' sales in inventory | 72.5 days |
| Merchandise inventory turnover | 6.3 times |
| Inventory turnover in days | 62.5 days |

The estimated operating cycle for 2001 is:

a.   70.9 days.
b.   135.0 days.
c.   96.9 days.
d.   99.0 days.
e.   none of the above.

_____ 19. If a firm has pledged its inventory, then the best indicator of its short-term liquidity may be indicated by:

a.   working capital.
b.   current ratio.
c.   acid-test ratio.
d.   inventory turnover.
e.   cash ratio.

_____ 20. Which of the following statements is **not** true?

    a. Investments classified as marketable securities should be long-term.
    b. To qualify as a marketable security, the investment must be readily marketable.
    c. For a security to be classified as a marketable security, its liquidity must be determined.
    d. Many companies do not disclose the detail of the marketable securities accounts.
    e. None of the above.

_____ 21. Szabo Company presented the following data for the most recent year:

| | |
|---|---|
| Current ratio | 2.0 |
| Quick or acid-test ratio | 1.5 |
| Current liabilities | $600,000 |
| Inventory turnover | 4 times |

Note: Compute the acid-test ratio using

$$\frac{\text{Current Assets} - \text{Inventory}}{\text{Current Liabilities}}$$

The inventory was:
a. $ 600,000
b. $1,200,000
c. $ 300,000
d. $ 900,000
e. $1,500,000

Questions 22-26 are based on the following information:

Fink Company's working capital accounts at December 31, 199X, are given below:

|  |  |  |
|---|---:|---:|
| **Current Assets:** |  |  |
| Cash |  | $ 150,000 |
| Marketable securities, lower of cost or market |  | 100,000 |
| Accounts receivable | $500,000 |  |
| Less allowance for doubtful accounts | 30,000 | 470,000 |
| Inventory, fifo |  | 500,000 |
| Prepaids |  | 20,000 |
| Total current assets |  | $1,240,000 |
|  |  |  |
| **Current Liabilities:** |  |  |
| Accounts payable |  | $ 500,000 |
| Notes payable |  | 60,000 |
| Taxes payable |  | 70,000 |
| Accrued liabilities |  | 40,000 |
| Total current liabilities |  | $ 670,000 |

Selected income statement accounts for the year ended December 31, 199X, are given below:

|  |  |
|---|---:|
| Net sales | $ 500,000 |
| Cost of goods sold | 300,000 |
| Selling and administrative expenses | 100,000 |

**Note:** The working capital at the end of the prior year was $600,000.

_____ 22. The working capital for December 31, 199X, is:

a. $570,000
b. $ 70,000
c. $740,000
d. $440,000
e. none of the above

_____ 23.   The current ratio for December 31, 199X, is:

        a.   2.48
        b.   1.85
        c.   1.00
        d.   1.45
        e.   none of the above

_____ 24.   The acid-test ratio for December 31 199X, is:

        a.   1.85
        b.   2.07
        c.   1.07
        d.    .37
        e.   none of the above

_____ 25.   The cash ratio for December 31, 199X, is:

        a.   1.85
        b.   2.07
        c.   1.07
        d.    .37
        e.   none of the above

_____ 26. The sales to working capital for the year ended
December 31, 199X, is:

a. 1.85
b. 1.07
c. .85
d. .07
e. none of the above


_____ 27. Aries Company presents the following data:

| | |
|---|---:|
| Accounts receivable, less allowance for doubtful accounts of $40,000 | $ 560,000 |
| Ending inventory | $ 700,000 |
| Net sales | $4,600,000 |
| Cost of goods sold | $3,300,000 |

The estimated time to realize cash from the ending
inventory is:

a. 120.00
b. 125.03
c. 130.03
d. 140.00
e. none of the above

Questions 28-29 are based on the following information:

Inflated Company has been using LIFO inventory. The company is required to disclose the replacement cost of its inventory and the replacement cost of its cost of goods sold on its annual statements. Selected data for the most recent year are as follows:

| | |
|---|---|
| Ending inventory, LIFO (estimated replacement cost $800,000) | $ 600,000 |
| Net sales | $1,000,000 |
| Cost of goods sold (estimated replacement cost $3,200,000) | $2,900,000 |

_____ 28. The days' sales in inventory, using the LIFO cost figure, is:

    a.   55.62
    b.   65.80
    c.   70.52
    d.   75.52
    e.   none of the above

_____ 29. The days' sales in inventory, using the replacement cost for the inventory and cost of goods sold, is:

    a.   81.25
    b.   91.25
    c.   101.25
    d.   98.00
    e.   none of the above

Questions 30-33 are based on the following information:

| Date | Description | Number of Units | Cost Per Unit | Total Cost |
|---|---|---|---|---|
| January 1 | Beginning inventory | 2,000 | $5.00 | $10,000 |
| March 10 | Purchase | 600 | 5.20 | 3,120 |
| April 5 | Purchase | 700 | 5.25 | 3,675 |
| August 20 | Purchase | 600 | 5.30 | 3,180 |
| November 10 | Purchase | 800 | 5.35 | 4,280 |
| December 20 | Purchase | 400 | 5.50 | 2,200 |
| | | 5,100 | | $26,455 |

A physical inventory at the end of the year indicates that 400 units are on hand and that they came from the November purchase. The company uses a periodic inventory system.

_____ 30. The cost of the inventory at the end of the year, using FIFO, is:

a. $2,120
b. $2,140
c. $2,200
d. $2,080
e. none of the above

_____ 31. The cost of the inventory at the end of the year, using LIFO, is:

a. $2,400
b. $1,800
c. $2,200
d. $2,000
e. none of the above

_____ 32.   The cost of the inventory at the end of the year,
              using weighted average cost, is:

              a.   $2,200
              b.   $2,000
              c.   $2,076
              d.   $2,100
              e.   none of the above

_____ 33.   The cost of the inventory at the end of the year,
              using specific identification, is:

              a.   $2,140
              b.   $2,076
              c.   $2,000
              d.   $2,200
              e.   none of the above

Chapter 6 - Problem 3 - True/False

Indicate whether each of the following is true (T) or false (F)
in the space provided.

_____ 1.    Even an entity on a very profitable course will find
              itself bankrupt if it fails to meet its obligations to
              short-term creditors.

_____ 2.    Compensating balances reduce the amount of cash
              available to the borrower to meet obligations and they
              decrease the effective interest rate for the borrower.

_____ 3. In terms of liquidity, it is to management's advantage to show investments under marketable securities instead of long-term investments.

_____ 4. The liquidity of a company that uses a natural business year tends to be overstated in comparison with a company that uses a calendar year.

_____ 5. In general, generally accepted accounting principles do not require unrealized losses to be reported on the income statement for long-term investments.

_____ 6. All equity securities should be classified as marketable securities.

_____ 7. Estimating the collectibility of any individual receivable is difficult, but estimating the collectibility of a group of receivables is usually even more difficult.

_____ 8. The charge-off of a specific account receivable influences the income statement and the net receivables on the balance sheet (allowance method in use).

_____ 9. The direct write-off method usually results in the proper matching of bad debt expense with revenue.

_____ 10. When a company has receivables classified as current, based upon industry practice, special note should be made of this when comparing with competitors.

_____ 11. Customer concentration will usually add an increased quality factor to receivables.

_____ 12. An increase in days' sales in receivables indicates an improvement in the control of receivables.

_____ 13. A shortening of the credit terms is an indication that there will be less risk in the collection of future receivables, while a lengthening of the credit terms is an indication that there will be a greater risk in the collection of future receivables.

_____ 14. Since the net sales figure includes both collectible and uncollectible accounts (gross sales), the comparable receivables figure should include gross receivables.

_____ 15. Ratios that indicate the liquidity of receivables can be misleading if sales are seasonal and/or the company uses a natural business year.

_____ 16. The company with the natural business year would tend to understate accounts receivable turnover, thus understating its liquidity.

_____ 17. In order to have a realistic indication of the liquidity of receivables, only the credit sales should be included in a computation of accounts receivable turnover.

_____ 18. Inventory levels are particularly sensitive to changes in business activity.

_____ 19. Under inflationary conditions, the cash flow to a firm using fifo is greater than the cash flow under lifo by the difference in the resulting tax between the two methods.

_____ 20. Lifo is ideal for a firm that has a high inventory turnover rate.

_____ 21. The days' sales in inventory is an estimate of the number of days that it will take to sell the current inventory.

_____ 22. A low sales to working capital ratio tentatively indicates an unprofitable use of working capital.

_____ 23. The cash ratio is usually the best indication of the firm's ability to pay current bills.

_____ 24. The collection of accounts receivable does not change the current ratio or the net working capital. The company is using the allowance method.

_____ 25. If current assets exceed current liabilities, payments to creditors will increase the current ratio.

# Chapter 6 - Problem 4 - Matching Computation of Ratios

Listed below are several ratios.  Match the letter that goes with each formula.

a.  days' sales in receivables
b.  accounts receivable turnover
c.  accounts receivable turnover in days
d.  days' sales in inventory
e.  inventory turnover
f.  inventory turnover in days

g.  operating cycle
h.  working capital
i.  current ratio
j.  acid-test ratio
k.  cash ratio
l.  sales to working capital

_____ 1.  $$\frac{\text{Sales}}{\text{Average Working Capital}}$$

_____ 2.  $$\frac{\text{Net Sales}}{\text{Average Gross Receivables}}$$

_____ 3.  Current Assets - Current Liabilities

_____ 4.  $$\frac{\text{Cash Equivalents + Marketable Securities + Net Receivables}}{\text{Current Liabilities}}$$

_____ 5.  $$\frac{\text{Gross Receivables}}{\text{Net Sales}/365}$$

_____ 6.  $$\frac{\text{Average Gross Receivables}}{\text{Net Sales}/365}$$

_____ 7.  $$\frac{\text{Average Inventory}}{\text{Cost of Goods Sold}/365}$$

_____ 8.  $$\frac{\text{Cash Equivalents + Marketable Securities}}{\text{Current Liabilities}}$$

_____ 9.  $$\frac{\text{Current Assets}}{\text{Current Liabilities}}$$

_____ 10.  $$\frac{\text{Accounts Receivable}}{\text{Turnover in Days}} + \frac{\text{Inventory Turnover}}{\text{in Days}}$$

_____ 11.  $$\frac{\text{Cost of Goods Sold}}{\text{Average Inventory}}$$

_____ 12. $\dfrac{\text{Ending Inventory}}{\text{Cost of Goods Sold}/365}$

## Chapter 6 - Problem 5 - Effect of Selected Transactions on Liquidity Ratios

Ajax Company's working capital accounts at December 31, 2000 are given below:

| | | |
|---|---:|---:|
| Current Assets | | |
| Cash | | $125,000 |
| Marketable securities | | 75,000 |
| Accounts receivable | $300,000 | |
| Less allowance for doubtful accounts | 30,000 | 270,000 |
| Inventory, lifo | | 450,000 |
| Prepaids | | 10,000 |
| Total current assets | | $930,000 |
| | | |
| Current Liabilities | | |
| Accounts payable | | $300,000 |
| Notes payable | | 50,000 |
| Taxes payable | | 40,000 |
| Accrued liabilities | | 35,500 |
| Total current liabilities | | $425,500 |

Selected income statement accounts for the year ended December 31, 2000 are given below:

| | |
|---|---:|
| Net sales | $3,000,000 |
| Cost of goods sold | 1,800,000 |
| Selling and administrative expenses | 350,000 |

For 2001, indicate the effect of each of the following transactions on working capital, current ratio, acid-test ratio and cash ratio. (The transactions are independent and take place at the beginning of 2001.) Give the effect in terms of +, -, or none. Consider each transaction to be the first transaction of the year. Assume at the start of the year that the current ratio is over 2 to 1, the acid test ratio is over 1 to 1, and the cash ratio is less than 1 to 1.

| Transaction | Working Capital | Current Ratio | Acid-Test Ratio | Cash Ratio |
|---|---|---|---|---|
| a. Sold marketable securities costing $15,000 for $15,000 cash | | | | |
| b. Paid accounts payable in the amount of $10,000 | | | | |
| c. Declared a cash dividend in the amount of $30,000 | | | | |
| d. Paid the above cash dividend | | | | |
| e. Purchased fixed assets for cash, $10,000 | | | | |
| f. Sold inventory costing $20,000 for $25,000 cash | | | | |
| g. Wrote off an account receivable in the amount of $10,000 | | | | |

Chapter 6 - Problem 6 - Review of Receivables for a Seasonal
Business

The Hickory store does 80% of its business between Thanksgiving
and Christmas, selling on 90-days credit.  Sales and receivables
data for the period ended December 31, 2001, and for the period
ended July 31, 2001, follow:

|  | For Period Ended December 31, 2001 | For Period Ended July 31, 2001 |
|---|---|---|
| Net sales | $1,200,000 | $1,180,000 |
| Receivables, less allowance for doubtful accounts: Beginning of period (allowance, January 1, 8,000; August 1, 5,000) | 260,000 | 95,000 |
| End of period (allowance December 31, 7,500; July 31, 4,800) | 250,000 | 100,000 |

**Required:**  a.  Compute the days' sales in receivables for July
31, 2001, and December 31, 2001.

b.  Compute the accounts receivable turnover for the
period ended July 31, 2001, and December 31, 2001.

c.  Comment on the results in (a) and (b).

# Chapter 6 - Problem 7 - Computation of Liquidity Ratios

A partial balance sheet and income statement for Toledo Corporation are as follows:

Toledo Corporation
Partial Balance Sheet
December 31, 2001

## Assets
Current assets:

| | |
|---|---:|
| Cash | $ 325,000 |
| Marketable securities | 380,000 |
| Receivables, less allowance of $4,000 | 420,000 |
| Inventories, LIFO | 700,000 |
| Prepaid expenses | 30,000 |
| Total current assets | $1,855,000 |

## Liabilities
Current liabilities:

| | |
|---|---:|
| Accounts payable | $ 300,000 |
| Notes payable | 350,000 |
| Accrued expenses | 60,000 |
| Income taxes payable | 30,000 |
| Total current liabilities | $ 740,000 |

Toledo Corporation
Partial Income Statement
For the Year Ended December 31, 2001

| | |
|---|---:|
| Net sales | $4,850,000 |
| | |
| Costs and expenses: | |
| Cost of sales | 3,400,000 |
| Selling, general, and administrative expenses | 380,000 |
| Interest expense | 18,000 |
| Income taxes | 400,000 |
| | 4,198,000 |
| Net income | $ 652,000 |

Note: The receivables at December 31, 2000, were $380,000, less an allowance of $6,000, for a gross receivables figure of $386,000. The inventory at December 31, 2000, was $600,000.

**Required:** Compute the following:
- a. Working capital
- b. Current ratio
- c. Acid-test ratio
- d. Cash ratio
- e. Days' sales in receivables
- f. Accounts receivable turnover in days
- g. Days' sales in inventory
- h. Inventory turnover in days
- i. Operating cycle

Chapter 6 - Problem 8 - Inventory Cost and Cost of Sales

The following are the inventory records of Fox Company:

|  | Units | Cost | Total |
|---|---|---|---|
| January 1 | 30 | $12 | $360 |
| Purchases: | | | |
| February 20 | 40 | 13 | 520 |
| July 10 | 50 | 14 | 700 |
| November 5 | 60 | 15 | 900 |
| December 15 | 20 | 17 | 340 |

Ending inventory consists of 18 units from the July purchase.

Note: The company uses a periodic inventory system.

**Required:** Calculate ending inventory and cost of sales, using: (a) FIFO, (b) LIFO, (c) average, and (d) specific identification.

Chapter 6 - Problem 9 - Determine The Cost of Sales

Granville Company had the financial data given below:

| | |
|---|---|
| Current ratio | 2.8 to 1 |
| *Acid test ratio | 2.3 to 1 |
| Current liabilities | $600,000 |
| Inventory turnover (using ending inventory) | 5 times |

*Assume that the acid-test ratio is computed as follows:

$$\frac{\text{Current Assets - Inventory}}{\text{Current Liabilities}}$$

**Required:**   Determine the cost of goods sold.

**CHAPTER 6 - SOLUTIONS**

Chapter 6 - Problem 1 - Supply the Words Necessary to Complete
                  the Following Items

1.  short-term; long-term

2.  operating cycle; one year; longer

3.  marketable securities; receivables, inventories

4.  operating cycle; cash

5.  accept; accept

6.  restrictions; deposit; current

7.  obligations; effective interest

8.  valuation; liquidity

9.  marketable; cash; operating cycle; longer

10. advantage; marketable securities, liquidity

11. conservative; investments

12. temporary

13. valuation; current assets

14. expense; year; matching

15. accounts receivable

16. longer; interest-bearing

17. fair value; present value

18. period of sale

19. industry practice; competitors

20. quality

21. collected; not

22. accounts receivable; sales

23. credit terms; receivables

24. seasonal; natural business

25. credit; liquidity

26. Inventory; short-term

27. cost

28. sale, used, consumed

29. trading, manufacturing

30. first-in, first-out; last-in, first-out

31. fifo; lifo

32. days; sell

33. misleading; natural business

34. inventory; operating cycle

35. costs, consumed, current assets

36. liquidation, current assets

37. current liabilities

38. current liabilities

39. working capital

40. current assets

41. cash

42. sales

43. cost; market

44. down; cost

45. quality; opinion

46. unprofitable

# Chapter 6 - Problem 2 - Multiple Choice

___a___   1.   The tire manufacturer would probably have the longest operating cycle.

___b___   2.   The winery business would probably have an operating cycle that is longer than a year.

___d___   3.  
$$\frac{\text{Gross Receivables}}{\text{Net Sales}/365} = \frac{\$325,200 + \$16,500}{\$3,180,000/365}$$

$$\frac{\$341,700}{\$8,712.33} = 39.2$$

___a___   4.   A material amount of sales on a cash basis would make receivables appear to be low.

___e___   5.  
$$\frac{\text{Net Sales}}{\text{Average Gross Receivables}}$$

2001

$$\frac{\$3,605,500}{(\$328,500 + \$18,200 + \$348,200 + \$15,100)/2}$$

$$\frac{\$3,605,600}{\$355,000} = 10.16$$

2000

$$\frac{\$3,120,500}{(\$348,200 + \$15,100 + \$258,000 + \$14,000)/2}$$

$$\frac{\$3,120,500}{\$317,650} = 9.82$$

___d___   6.  
$$\frac{\text{Ending Inventory}}{\text{Cost of Goods Sold}/365}$$

2001

$$\frac{\$456,500}{\$3,100,000/365} \qquad \frac{\$456,500}{\$8,493.15} = 53.75$$

135

2000

$$\frac{\$426,500}{\$3,000,000/365} \qquad \frac{\$426,500}{\$8,219.18} = 51.89$$

b    7.   Cost Of Goods Sold
              Average Inventory

2001

$$\frac{\$4,250,000}{(\$655,000 + \$630,000)/2} = \frac{\$4,250,000}{\$642,500} = 6.61$$

2000

$$\frac{\$3,975,000}{(\$630,000 + \$580,000)/2} = \frac{\$3,975,000}{\$605,000} = 6.57$$

c    8.   Current liabilities are those obligations whose liquidation expects to require the use of current assets or the creation of other current liabilities within the normal operating cycle or one year, whichever is longer. Preferred stock does not fall within this guideline.

e    9.   A contingent liability that has not been recorded could result in a payment, reducing the liquidity position.

a    10.   Company B uses fifo for inventory valuation. This would result in higher profit in times of inflation. Company B has the higher inventory amount, which would lower the indicated inventory turnover.

d    11.   An increasing inventory could increase the current ratio. Inventory is not part of the quick ratio. Thus, an increasing current ratio with a declining quick ratio could indicate that the firm is carrying excess inventory.

d    12.   A bakery selling retail only would likely have a very short operating, fast turnover of inventory and likely no receivables.

a 13. $\dfrac{\text{Gross Receivables}}{\text{Net Sales}/365}$

$$\dfrac{\$300,000 + \$10,000}{\$2,800,000/365} = \dfrac{\$310,000}{\$7,671.23} = 40.4$$

e 14. $\dfrac{\text{Net Sales}}{\text{Average Gross Receivables}}$

$$\dfrac{\$26,500,000}{(\$2,520,000 + \$120,000 + \$2,700,000 + \$120,000)/2} = 9.71$$

c 15. $\dfrac{\text{Average Gross Receivables}}{\text{Net Sales}/365}$

$$\dfrac{(\$2,520,000 + \$120,000 + \$2,700,000 + \$120,000)/2}{\$26,500,000/365}$$

$$\dfrac{\$2,730,000}{\$72,602.74} = 37.60$$

d 16. $\dfrac{\text{Cost of Goods Sold}}{\text{Average Inventory}} = \dfrac{\$3,000,000}{(\$500,000 + \$450,000)/2} = 6.32$

a 17. $\dfrac{\text{Average Inventory}}{\text{Cost of Goods Sold}/365}$

$$\dfrac{(\$450,000 + \$500,000)/2}{\$3,000,000/365}$$

$$\dfrac{\$475,000}{\$8,219.18} = 57.79$$

c 18. Accounts Receivable + Inventory Turnover
Turnover In Days     In Days

       34.4       +      62.5        = 96.9

_c_ 19. Since inventory has been pledged, working capital, current ratio and inventory turnover may not be good indicators of liquidity. The acid-test ratio is normally considered to be a better indicator of liquidity than the cash ratio.

_a_ 20. Investments classified as marketable securities should be short-term.

_c_ 21. $\dfrac{\text{Current Assets}}{\$600,000} = 2.0$

Current Assets = $1,200,000

$\dfrac{\$1,200,000 - \text{Inventory}}{\$600,000} = 1.5$

$1,200,000 - Inventory = $900,000

Inventory = $300,000

_a_ 22. Current Assets - Current Liabilities
$1,240,000     - $670,000        = $570,000

_b_ 23. $\dfrac{\text{Current Assets}}{\text{Current Liabilities}} = \dfrac{\$1,240,000}{\$670,000} = 1.85$

_c_ 24. $\dfrac{\text{Cash Equivalents+Marketable Securities+Net Receivables}}{\text{Current Liabilities}}$

$\dfrac{\$150,000 + \$100,000 + \$470,000}{\$670,000} = \dfrac{\$720,000}{\$670,000} = 1.07$

_d_ 25. $\dfrac{\text{Cash Equivalents+Marketable Securities}}{\text{Current Liabilities}}$

$\dfrac{\$150,000 + 100,000}{\$670,000} = \dfrac{\$250,000}{\$670,000} = .37$

_c_ 26. $\dfrac{\text{Sales}}{\text{Average Working Capital}}$

$\dfrac{\$500,000}{(\$1,240,000 - \$670,000 + \$600,000)/2} = \dfrac{\$500,000}{\$585,000} = .85$

__b__ 27.  Days' Sales In  +  Days' Sales In
          Receivables        Inventory

$$\frac{\text{Gross Receivables}}{\text{Net Sales}/365} + \frac{\text{Ending Inventory}}{\text{Cost Of Goods Sold}/365}$$

$$\frac{\$560,000 + \$40,000}{\$4,600,000/365} + \frac{\$700,000}{\$3,300,000/365}$$

$$\frac{\$600,000}{\$12,602.74} + \frac{\$700,000}{\$9,041.10}$$

$$47.61 + 77.42 = 125.03$$

__d__ 28.  $$\frac{\text{Ending Inventory}}{\text{Cost of Goods Sold}/365} = \frac{\$600,000}{\$2,900,000 / 365} = 75.52$$

__b__ 29.  $$\frac{\text{Ending Inventory}}{\text{Cost Of Goods Sold}/365}$$

$$\frac{\$800,000}{\$3,200,000/365} = \frac{\$800,000}{\$8,767.12} = 91.25$$

__c__ 30.  400 x $5.50 = $2,200

__d__ 31.  400 x $5.00 = $2,000

__c__ 32.  400 x $5.19 = $2,076

          Average: $$\frac{\$26,455}{5,100} = \$5.19$$

__a__ 33.  400 x $5.35 = $2,140

Chapter 6 - Problem 3 - True/False

| | | | | | | |
|---|---|---|---|---|---|
| __T__ | 1. | __F__ | 9. | __T__ | 17. |
| __F__ | 2. | __T__ | 10. | __T__ | 18. |
| __T__ | 3. | __F__ | 11. | __F__ | 19. |
| __T__ | 4. | __F__ | 12. | __F__ | 20. |
| __T__ | 5. | __T__ | 13. | __T__ | 21. |
| __F__ | 6. | __T__ | 14. | __T__ | 22. |
| __F__ | 7. | __T__ | 15. | __F__ | 23. |
| __F__ | 8. | __F__ | 16. | __T__ | 24. |
| | | | | __T__ | 25. |

## Chapter 6 - Problem 4 - Matching Computation of Ratios

| | | | | | |
|---|---|---|---|---|---|
| l | 1. | a | 5. | i | 9. |
| b | 2. | c | 6. | g | 10. |
| h | 3. | f | 7. | e | 11. |
| j | 4. | k | 8. | d | 12. |

## Chapter 6 - Problem 5 - Effect of Selected Transactions on Liquidity Ratios

| Transaction | Working Capital | Current Ratio | Acid-Test Ratio | Cash Ratio |
|---|---|---|---|---|
| a. | None | None | None | None |
| b. | None | - | - | - |
| c. | - | - | - | - |
| d. | None | + | + | + |
| e. | - | - | - | - |
| f. | + | + | + | + |
| g. | None | None | None | None |

## Chapter 6 - Problem 6 - Review of Receivables for A Seasonal Business

a.  Days' Sales In Receivables = $\dfrac{\text{Gross Receivables}}{\text{Net Sales}/365}$

$$\text{December 31, 2001} = \frac{\$250,000 + \$7,500}{\$1,200,000/365} = 78.32 \text{ Days}$$

$$\text{July 31, 2001} = \frac{\$100,000 + \$4,800}{\$1,180,000/365} = 32.42 \text{ Days}$$

b.  Accounts Receivable Turnover = $\dfrac{\text{Net Sales}}{\text{Average Gross Receivable}}$

$$\text{December 31, 2001} = \frac{\$1,200,000}{(\$260,000 + \$8,000 + \$250,000 + \$7,500)/2}$$

$$= 4.57$$

$$\text{July 31, 2001} = \frac{\$1,180,000}{(\$100,000 + \$4,800 + \$95,000 + \$5,000)/2}$$

$$= 11.52$$

c.  This company appears to have a seasonal business because of the materially different days' sales in receivables and accounts receivable turnover when computed at the two different dates.  The ratios computed will not be meaningful in an absolute sense but they would be meaningful in a comparative sense when comparing the same dates from year to year, but they would not be meaningful when comparing different dates.

Chapter 6 - Problem 7 - Computation of Liquidity Ratios

a.  Working Capital = Current Assets - Current Liabilities
$1,855,000 - $740,000 = $1,115,000

b.  Current Ratio = $\dfrac{\text{Current Assets}}{\text{Current Liabilities}} = \dfrac{\$1,855,000}{\$740,000} = 2.51$

c.  Acid-Test Ratio = $\dfrac{\text{Cash Equivalents + Net Receivables + Marketable Securities}}{\text{Current Liabilities}}$

$\dfrac{\$325,000 + \$380,000 + \$420,000}{\$740,000} = 1.52$

d.  Cash Ratio = $\dfrac{\text{Cash Equivalents + Marketable Securities}}{\text{Current Liabilities}}$

$\dfrac{\$325,000 + \$380,000}{\$740,000} = .95$

e.  Days' Sales in Receivables = $\dfrac{\text{Gross Receivables}}{\text{Net Sales}/365}$

$\dfrac{\$420,000 + \$4,000}{\$4,850,000/365} = 31.91$

f.  Accounts Receivable Turnover In Days = $\dfrac{\text{Average Gross Receivables}}{\text{Net Sales}/365}$

$\dfrac{(\$420,000 + \$4,000 + \$380,000 + \$6,000)/2}{\$4,850,000/365} = 30.48$

g. Days' Sales In Inventory = $\dfrac{\text{Ending Inventory}}{\text{Cost of Goods Sold}/365}$

$$\dfrac{\$700,000}{\$3,400,000/365} = 75.15$$

h. Inventory Turnover in Days = $\dfrac{\text{Average Inventory}}{\text{Cost of Goods Sold}/365}$

$$\dfrac{(\$700,000 + \$600,000)/2}{\$3,400,000/365} = 69.78$$

i. Operating Cycle = $\dfrac{\text{Accounts Receivable}}{\text{Turnover in Days}} + \dfrac{\text{InventoryTurnover}}{\text{InDays}}$

  $30.48 + 69.78 = 100.26$

Chapter 6 - Problem 8 - Inventory Cost and Cost of Sales

|  | Ending Inventory | | Cost of Sales | |
|---|---|---|---|---|
| a. | FIFO | | | |
|  | 18 x $17 = | $306 | 30 x $12 = | $   360 |
|  | | | 40 x $13 = | 520 |
|  | | | 50 x $14 = | 700 |
|  | | | 60 x $15 = | 900 |
|  | | | 2 x $17 = | 34 |
|  | | | | $2,514 |
| b. | LIFO | | | |
|  | 18 x $12 = | $216 | 12 x $12 = | $   144 |
|  | | | 40 x $13 = | 520 |
|  | | | 50 x $14 = | 700 |
|  | | | 60 x $15 = | 900 |
|  | | | 20 x $17 = | 340 |
|  | | | | $2,604 |
| c. | Average | | | |
|  | 30 x $12 = | $   360 | $2,820/200 = $14.10 | |
|  | 40 x $13 = | 520 | | |
|  | 50 x $14 = | 700 | | |
|  | 60 x $15 = | 900 | | |
|  | 20 x $17 = | 340 | | |
|  | 200 | $2,820 | | |

| Inventory | Cost of Sales |
|---|---|
| 18 x $14.10 = $253.80 | 182 x $14.10 = $2,566.20 |

d.  Specific Identification
        18 x $14 = $252            30 x $12 =   $   360
                                   40 x $13 =       520
                                   32 x $14 =       448
                                   60 x $15 =       900
                                   20 x $17 =       340
                                                $2,568

Chapter 6 - Problem 9 - Determine The Cost of Sales

Current Ratio = $\dfrac{\text{Current Assets}}{\text{Current Liabilities}} = \dfrac{X}{\$600,000} = 2.8$

Current assets = ($600,000)x(2.8) = $1,680,000

Acid-Test Ratio = $\dfrac{\text{Current Assets - Inventory}}{\text{Current Liabilities}} = \dfrac{\$1,680,000 - X}{\$600,000}$

= 2.3

$1,680,000 - X = $1,380,000
        - X = $1,380,000 - $1,680,000
          X = $300,000 (inventory)

Inventory Turnover = $\dfrac{\text{Cost of Goods Sold}}{\text{Inventory}} = \dfrac{X}{\$300,000} = 5$

Cost of goods sold = $1,500,000

# Chapter 7: Long-Term Debt-Paying Ability

Chapter 7 - Problem 1 - Supply the Words Necessary to Complete
the Following Items

1.  In the long run, there is usually a relationship between the
    _____ _____ that is the result of accrual accounting
    and the ability of the firm to meet its _____-_____
    obligations.

2.  The _____ of the firm is not considered important
    in determining the _____-_____ debt-paying ability, since
    _____ is the end result of _____ accounting.

3.  When the interest rate is _____, there is the added _____
    that the company will not be able to earn more on the funds
    than the interest _____ on them.

4.  Capitalization of interest results in interest being _____
    to a fixed asset instead of being _____.

5.  To get a better indication of a firm's ability to cover
    _____ payments in the _____ run, the noncash charges
    for _____, _____, and _____ can be
    added back to the numerator of the times interest _____
    ratio.

6.  Operating leases are not reflected on the balance sheet, but
    they are reflected on the _____ _____ in the _____
    _____.

7.  The debt ratio indicates the percentage of assets that were
    financed by _____.

8.  The reserve accounts classified under liabilities result
    from an _____ charge to the _____ _____ and an
    equal increase in the reserve account on the _____
    _____.

9.  Reserve accounts do _____ represent definite commitments to
    pay out _____ in the future.

10. Taxes payable represents actual current _____ _____,
    which are determined by the tax _____.

11. The short-term deferred tax account will be classified as a
    _____ _____ or _____ _____, depending on the
    nature of the temporary differences _____ in the next
    year.

12. Revenue and expense items that never go on the tax return
    are referred to as _____ differences.

13. The account _____ _____ interest results when
    the firm has _____ another company of which it owns
    less than _____.

14. Redeemable preferred stock is subject to _____
    _____ requirements or has a _____ feature that
    is outside the control of the issuer.

15. Leases are handled by the lessee by _____ the lease
    or by reporting it as an _____ lease.

16. A capitalized lease is handled as if the lessee _____ the
    asset. The leased asset is in the _____ _____ and the
    related obligation is included in _____.

17. Operating leases are not reflected on the _____ _____,
    but they are reflected in a footnote and the income
    statement in the _____ _____.

18. If these leases had been capitalized, the amount added to
    _____ _____ and the amount added to _____ would
    be the same at the time of the initial entry.

19. When an employee is _____ in the pension plan, she or he
    is eligible to receive some pension benefits at _____
    regardless of whether the employee continues working for the
    _____.

20. A company-sponsored pension plan is either a _____
    _____ plan or a _____ _____ plan.

21. A _____ pension benefit is one that the employee is
    entitled to even if he or she leaves the firm prior to
    _____.

22. Beginning in 1993, most firms must accrue or set up a
    reserve for future medical benefits of _____, rather
    than _____ these costs when _____.

23. A _____ _____ is an association of two or more businesses established for a special purpose.

24. A _____ is characterized by an existing condition, uncertainty as to the ultimate effect, and its resolution depending on one or more _____ events.

25. When examining financial statements, a footnote that describes contingencies should be closely reviewed to be aware of possible significant _____ that are ____ disclosed on the face of the _____ _____.

26. Disclosure of matters relating to off-balance-sheet _____ _____ and _____ _____ concentrations are required.

## Chapter 7 - Problem 2 - Multiple Choice

Choose the best answer for each of the following questions and enter the identifying letter in the space provided.

_____ 1. Which of the following ratios can be used as a guide to a firm's ability to carry debt from an income perspective?

      a. Debt Ratio
      b. Debt to Tangible Net Worth
      c. Debt/Equity
      d. Times Interest Earned
      e. Current Ratio

_____ 2. There is substantial disagreement on all but one of the following items as to whether it should be considered a liability in the debt ratio:

      a. short-term liabilities
      b. reserve accounts
      c. deferred taxes
      d. minority shareholders' interest
      e. preferred stock

_____ 3. A firm may have substantial liabilities that are **not** disclosed on the face of the balance sheet from all but one of the following:

   a. leases
   b. pension plans
   c. joint ventures
   d. contingencies
   e. bonds payable

_____ 4. Which of the following will cause times interest earned to drop?

   a. an increase in bonds payable with no change in operating income
   b. a decrease in preferred stock dividends
   c. a decrease in cost of goods sold with no change in operating income
   d. a rise in sales with an increase in operating income
   e. a decrease in interest rates

_____ 5. In computing the debt ratio, which of the following is subtracted in the denominator?

   a. copyrights
   b. trademarks
   c. patents
   d. marketable securities
   e. none of the above

_____ 6. All but one of these ratios are considered to be debt ratios:

   a. times interest earned
   b. debt ratio
   c. debt/equity
   d. fixed charge ratio
   e. current ratio

_____ 7. Which of the following statements is **false**?

    a.  The debt to tangible net worth ratio is more conservative than the debt ratio.
    b.  The debt to tangible net worth ratio is more conservative than the debt/equity ratio.
    c.  Times interest earned indicates an income statement view of debt.
    d.  The debt/equity ratio indicates an income statement view of debt.
    e.  The debt ratio indicates a balance sheet view of debt.

_____ 8. Sneider Company has long-term debt of $500,000, while Abbott Company has long-term debt of $50,000. Which of the following statements best represents an analysis of the long-term debt position of these two firms?

    a.  Sneider Company's times interest earned should be lower than Abbott Company's.
    b.  Abbott Company's times interest earned should be lower than Sneider Company's.
    c.  Abbott Company has a better long-term borrowing ability than does Sneider Company.
    d.  Sneider Company has a better long-term borrowing ability than does Abbott Company.
    e.  none of the above.

_____ 9. Fox Company had the following financial statistics for 2002:

| | |
|---|---|
| Long-term debt | $600,000 |
| Interest expense | 50,000 |
| Capitalized interest | 8,000 |
| Net income | 63,000 |
| Income tax | 55,000 |

What is the times interest earned for 2002?

    a.  2.36
    b.  1.95
    c.  2.90
    d.  3.36
    e.  none of the above

_____ 10. A times interest earned ratio of .20 to 1 means:

   a. that the firm will default on its interest payment.
   b. that net income is less than the interest expense (including capitalized interest).
   c. that cash flow exceeds the net income.
   d. that the firm should reduce its debt.
   e. none of the above.

_____ 11. Szabo Company reports the following (liabilities and stockholders' equity) capital at December 31, 2002:

| | |
|---|---|
| Current liabilities | $200,000 |
| Long-term debt | 500,000 |
| Deferred income taxes | 20,000 |
| Preferred stock | 90,000 |
| Premium on preferred stock | 10,000 |
| Common stock | 250,000 |
| Premium on common stock | 30,000 |
| Retained earnings | 200,000 |
| Treasury stock | 50,000 |

What is the debt ratio?

   a. .60
   b. .58
   c. .53
   d. .55
   e. none of the above

_____ 12. The following accounts relate to Melcher Company at December 31, 2002:

| | (In millions) |
|---|---|
| Current liabilities | $ 8.9 |
| Bonds payable | 14.0 |
| Minority interest | 2.0 |
| Common stock | 10.0 |
| Retained earnings | 18.0 |
| Treasury stock | 2.0 |

What is the debt-equity ratio?

   a. .881
   b. .958
   c. .830
   d. .900
   e. none of the above

_____ 13. In computing debt to tangible net worth, which of the following is **not** subtracted in the denominator?

    a.  patents
    b.  goodwill
    c.  land
    d.  bonds payable
    e.  c and d

_____ 14. The ratio fixed charge coverage:

    a.  is a cash flow indication of debt-paying ability.
    b.  is an income statement indication of debt-paying ability.
    c.  is a balance sheet indication of debt-paying ability.
    d.  will usually be higher than the times interest earned ratio.
    e.  none of the above.

_____ 15. Under the Employee Retirement Income Security Act, a company can be liable for its pension plan up to:

    a.  30 percent of its net worth.
    b.  30 percent of pension liabilities.
    c.  30 percent of liabilities.
    d.  40 percent of its net worth.
    e.  none of the above.

_____ 16. Which of the following statements is correct?

    a.  Capitalized interest should be included with interest expense when computing times interest earned.
    b.  A ratio that indicates a firm's long-term debt-paying ability from the balance sheet view is the times interest earned.
    c.  Some of the items on the income statement that are excluded in order to compute times interest earned are interest expense, income taxes, and interest income.
    d.  Usually the highest times interest coverage in the most recent five-year period is used as the primary indication of the interest coverage.
    e.  none of the above.

_____ 17.   Which of these items does **not** represent a definite
           commitment to pay out funds in the future?

           a.   notes payable
           b.   bonds payable
           c.   minority shareholders' interests
           d.   wages payable
           e.   none of the above

Questions 18-19 are based on the following information:

| | |
|---|---:|
| Net sales | $2,400,000 |
| **Costs and deductions:** | |
| Cost of sales | 1,600,000 |
| Selling and administrative expenses | 200,000 |
| Interest expense | 60,000 |
| Income taxes | 230,000 |
| | 2,090,000 |
| | $ 310,000 |

Note:  Depreciation expense totals $200,000.

_____ 18.   The times interest earned is:

           a.   40.1
           b.   60.0
           c.   30.5
           d.   10.0
           e.   none of the above

_____ 19.   The cash-basis times interest earned is:

           a.   18.0
           b.   20.0
           c.   10.0
           d.   13.3
           e.   none of the above

Questions 20-21 are based on the following information:

| | |
|---|---|
| Net sales | $1,800,000 |
| | |
| Cost and deductions: | |
| Cost of sales | 1,400,000 |
| Selling and administrative expenses | 250,000 |
| Interest expense | 50,000 |
| Income taxes | 20,000 |
| | 1,720,000 |
| | $ 80,000 |

Note: Depreciation expense totals $20,000, preferred dividends are $10,000, and operating lease payments are $30,000. Assume that 1/3 of operating lease payments is for interest.

_____ 20. The times interest earned is:

     a.   2.5
     b.   2.7
     c.   2.6
     d.   3.0
     e.   none of the above

_____ 21. The fixed charge coverage is:
     a.   2.00
     b.   2.52
     c.   3.10
     d.   2.67
     e.   none of the above

Questions 22-24 are based on the following information:

| Liabilities and shareholders' equity: | |
|---|---|
| Current liabilities | $ 70,000 |
| Long-term debt, 10% | 100,000 |
| Deferred income taxes | 20,000 |
| Minority interest | 15,000 |
| Shareholders' equity | 160,000 |
| Total liabilities and shareholders' equity | $365,000 |

Note: Intangibles totaled $40,000.

_____ 22.  The debt ratio is:

    a.  .40
    b.  .45
    c.  .56
    d.  .50
    e.  none of the above

_____ 23.  The debt/equity ratio is:

    a.  1.20
    b.  1.28
    c.   .56
    d.   .50
    e.  none of the above

_____ 24.  The debt to tangible net worth is:

    a.  1.20
    b.  1.28
    c.  1.71
    d.   .56
    e.  none of the above

## Chapter 7 - Problem 3 - True/False

Indicate whether each of the following is true (T) or false (F) in the space provided.

_____ 1.  A good record of times interest earned is indicated by a relatively high, stable coverage of interest over the years.

_____ 2.  High interest rates provide extraordinarily good opportunities for a firm to favorably "trade on the equity" (use of leverage).

_____ 3.  Capitalized interest represents a non-cash flow item that is added to the balance sheet.

_____ 4.  In the short-run, a firm can often meet its interest obligations even when the times interest earned is less than 1.

_____ 5.  Non-cash charges for depreciation, depletion, and amortization can be added back to the numerator of the times interest earned ratio in order to obtain a long-run indication of a firm's ability to carry interest payments.

_____ 6.  The fixed charge coverage is a more conservative ratio than the times interest earned ratio, as it relates to a firm's ability to carry debt.

_____ 7.  An operating lease for a relatively long term is a type of long-term financing.

_____ 8.  The account minority shareholders' interest results when a firm has not consolidated another company on which it owns less than 100%.

_____ 9.  In general, industries that have stable earnings can handle more debt than industries that have cyclical earnings.

_____ 10. Shareholders' equity is understated to the extent that assets have a value greater than book value.

_____ 11. The debt to tangible net worth ratio is a more conservative ratio than either the debt ratio or the debt/equity ratio.

_____ 12. A higher proportion of short-term debt in relation to long-term debt indicates a decreased risk in a firm's financial structure.

_____ 13. A firm may have assets that have substantial value greater than the amount indicated on the financial statements.

_____ 14. A reasonable determination of a firm's pension liabilities can be made by reviewing the liabilities disclosed on the face of the balance sheet.

_____ 15. All contingent liabilities are disclosed and recorded as liabilities.

_____ 16. Under generally accepted accounting principles, a manufacturing firm would not consolidate a bank, even when effective operating control is present.

_____ 17. A times interest earned ratio of .60 to 1.00 means that the firm will default on its interest payments.

_____ 18. When analyzing a firm's long-term debt-paying ability, we only want to determine the firm's ability to pay the interest.

_____ 19. The profitability of a firm is considered to be important in determining the short-term debt-paying ability of the firm.

_____ 20. A good times interest earned record would be indicated by a relatively high and floating coverage for the times interest earned coverage.

_____ 21. Equity earnings are included in earnings for the times interest earned coverage.

_____ 22. Liabilities are a definite commitment to pay out funds in the future.

_____ 23. The debt ratio is a more conservative ratio than the debt to tangible net worth.

_____ 24. All potential liabilities of a joint venture are on the face of the balance sheet of the parent company.

_____ 25. A defined contribution plan shifts the risk to the employee as to whether the pension funds will grow to provide for a reasonable pension payment upon retirement.

_____ 26. The lower the interest rate used, the lower the present value of the pension liability and the lower the immediate pension cost.

_____ 27. The declaration and payment of a cash dividend would not directly influence the times interest earned.

_____ 28. The declaration and payment of a stock dividend would not influence the times interest earned.

_____ 29. Conversion of bonds to common stock outstanding would increase the debt ratio.

_____ 30. The sale of common stock for cash would increase the debt/equity.

_____ 31. The sale of common stock for cash would not directly influence the times interest earned.

_____ 32. Repayment of a long-term bank loan would decrease the debt ratio.

_____ 33. Increases of profits by cutting the cost of sales would increase the times interest earned.

Listed below are several ratios.  Match the letter that goes with each formula.

a.   times interest earned
b.   fixed charge coverage
c.   debt ratio
d.   debt/equity ratio
e.   debt to tangible net worth


_____ 1.   $$\dfrac{\text{Total Liabilities}}{\text{Shareholders' Equity - Intangible Assets}}$$


_____ 2.   $$\dfrac{\text{Total Liabilities}}{\text{Total Assets}}$$


_____ 3.   $$\dfrac{\substack{\text{Recurring Earnings, Excluding Interest}\\\text{Expense, Tax Expense, Equity Earnings,}\\\text{and Minority Earnings}}}{\substack{\text{Interest Expense, Including}\\\text{Capitalized Interest}}}$$


_____ 4.   $$\dfrac{\substack{\text{Recurring Earnings, Excluding Interest}\\\text{Expense, Tax Expense, Equity Earnings,}\\\text{+ Interest Portion of Rentals}}}{\substack{\text{Interest Expense, Including Capitalized}\\\text{Interest + Interest Portion of Rentals}}}$$


_____ 5.   $$\dfrac{\text{Total Liabilities}}{\text{Shareholders' Equity}}$$

# Chapter 7 - Problem 5 - Matching Pension Plan Terms

Listed below are pension plan terms. Match the letter that goes with each term.

a. multi-employer pension plan
b. defined contribution plan
c. defined benefit plan
d. vested benefits
e. unvested benefits
f. prior service cost
g. accumulated benefit obligation
h. projected benefit obligation
i. net periodic pension cost

_____ 1. Pension plans maintained jointly by two or more unrelated employers.

_____ 2. A pension plan that defines the benefits to be received by the participants in the plan.

_____ 3. Entitles the employee to a benefit, even if he or she leaves the firm prior to retirement.

_____ 4. The actuarial present value of benefits attributed by the pension benefit formula to employee service rendered before a specified date and based on employee service and compensation (if applicable) prior to that date.

_____ 5. A pension benefit that accrues to the employee that the employee will lose if the employee leaves the firm prior to receiving a vested interest.

_____ 6. A credit to employees for years of service provided before the date of adoption or amendment of the pension plan.

_____ 7. The amount of net periodic pension cost for a period.

_____ 8. The actuarial present value as of a date of all benefits attributed by the pension benefit formula to employee service rendered prior to that date.

_____ 9. A pension plan that defines the contributions of the company to the pension plan.

# Chapter 7 - Problem 6 - Compute the Times Interest Earned and Fixed Charge Coverage

Loral Company reports the following statement of income:

| | |
|---|---:|
| Operating revenues | $60,000 |
| | |
| Costs and expenses: | |
| Cost of sales | 35,000 |
| Selling, service, administrative and general expense | 6,000 |
| | 41,000 |
| Income before interest expense and income taxes | 19,000 |
| Interest expense | 1,000 |
| Income before income taxes | 18,000 |
| Income taxes | 7,000 |
| Net income | $11,000 |

Note: Depreciation expense totals $2,000; preferred dividends total $200; operating lease payments total $600. Assume 1/3 of operating lease payments is for interest.

Required: a. Compute the times interest earned.
b. Compute the fixed charge coverage.

# Chapter 7 - Problem 7 - Computation of Debt Ratios

The following information is computed from the Jones Company annual report for 2002:

| | |
|---|---:|
| Current assets | $ 1,800 |
| Property and equipment, net | 8,000 |
| Intangible assets, at cost less applicable amortization | 300 |
| | $10,100 |
| | |
| Current liabilities | $ 1,000 |
| Deferred federal income taxes | 400 |
| Mortgage note payable | 1,900 |
| Stockholders' equity | 6,800 |
| | $10,100 |
| | |
| Net sales | $32,000 |
| Cost of goods sold | 24,000 |
| Selling and administrative expense | 3,600 |
| Interest expense | 180 |
| Income tax expense | 1,600 |
| Net income | $ 2,620 |

Note: One-third of the operating lease rental charges was interest of $600. Capitalized interest totaled $100.

**Required:** Compute the following ratios:
a. times interest earned
b. fixed charge coverage
c. debt ratio
d. debt/equity ratio
e. debt to tangible net worth

# CHAPTER 7 - SOLUTIONS

Chapter 7 - Problem 1 - Supply the Words Necessary to Complete
　　　　the Following Items

1.　reported income; long-term

2.　profitability; short-term; profitability; accrual

3.　high; risk; cost

4.　added, expensed

5.　interest; short; depreciation, depletion; amortization;
　　earned

6.　income statement; rent expense

7.　creditors

8.　expense; income statement; balance sheet

9.　not; funds

10.　taxes payable; return

11.　current asset; current liability; reversing

12.　permanent

13.　minority shareholders'; consolidated; 100%

14.　mandatory redemption; redemption

15.　capitalizing; operating

16.　bought; fixed assets; liabilities

17.　balance sheet; rent expense

18.　fixed assets; liabilities

19.　vested; retirement; employer

20.　defined contribution; defined benefit

21.　vested; retirement

22.　retirees, deduct; paid

23. joint venture

24. contingency; future

25. liabilities; not; balance sheet

26. financial instruments; credit risk

## Chapter 7 - Problem 2 - Multiple Choice

| | | |
|---|---|---|
| __d__ | 1. | The times interest earned ratio indicates a firm's long-term debt-paying ability from the income statement view. |
| __e__ | 2. | Preferred stock is owned by stockholders. |
| __e__ | 3. | The bonds payable liability will be shown on the balance sheet. |
| __a__ | 4. | The increase in bonds payable will increase interest expense. The increase in interest expense along with no change in operating income will result in a lower times interest earned. |
| __e__ | 5. | The denominator of the debt ratio is total assets. Therefore none of these assets are subtracted. |
| __e__ | 6. | The current ratio is considered to be a liquidity ratio. |
| __d__ | 7. | The debt/equity ratio represents a balance sheet view of debt. |
| __e__ | 8. | There is not adequate information to form an opinion on the long-term debt position. |
| __c__ | 9. | Recurring Earnings, Excluding Interest Expense, <u>Tax Expense, Equity Earnings, and Minority Earnings</u> Interest Expense, Including Capitalized Interest |

| | |
|---|---|
| Net income | $ 63,000 |
| Plus income tax | 55,000 |
| Plus interest expense | 50,000 |
| Adjusted Income | $168,000 |
| | |
| Interest expense | $ 50,000 |
| Capitalized interest | 8,000 |
| Total Interest | $ 58,000 |

$$\frac{\text{Adjusted Income}}{\text{Total Interest}} = \frac{\$168,000}{\$58,000} = 2.90$$

__b__ 10. With a times interest earned ratio of .20 to 1, net income is less than the interest expense.

__b__ 11. Liabilities:

| | |
|---|---:|
| Current liabilities | $ 200,000 |
| Long-term debt | 500,000 |
| Deferred income taxes | 20,000 |
| | $ 720,000 |

Stockholders' equity:

| | |
|---|---:|
| Preferred stock | $ 90,000 |
| Premium on preferred stock | 10,000 |
| Common stock | 250,000 |
| Premium on common stock | 30,000 |
| Retained earnings | 200,000 |
| Treasury stock | (50,000) |
| | $ 530,000 |
| Total liabilities and stockholders' equity (Also total assets) | $1,250,000 |

$$\frac{\text{Total Liabilities}}{\text{Total Assets}} = \frac{\$720,000}{\$1,250,000} = .58$$

__b__ 12. Liabilities:

| | |
|---|---:|
| Current liabilities | $ 8.9 |
| Bonds payable | 14.0 |
| Minority interest | 2.0 |
| Total liabilities | $24.9 |

Shareholders' equity:

| | |
|---|---:|
| Common stock | $10.0 |
| Retained earnings | 18.0 |
| Treasury stock | <2.0> |
| Total shareholders' equity | $26.0 |

$$\frac{\text{Total Liabilities}}{\text{Total Shareholders' Equity}} = \frac{\$24.9}{\$26.0} = .958$$

__e__ 13. Intangible assets are subtracted in the denominator. Land and bonds payable are not intangible assets.

__b__ 14. The ratio fixed charge coverage is an income statement indication of debt-paying ability.

a 15. The Employee Retirement Income Security Act calls for a company to be liable for its pension plan up to 30 percent of its net worth.

a 16. Capitalized interest should be included with interest expense when computing times interest earned.

c 17. Minority shareholders' interest does not represent a definite commitment to pay out funds in the future.

d 18. $\dfrac{\text{Recurring Earnings, Excluding Interest Expense, Tax Expense, Equity Earnings, and Minority Earnings}}{\text{Interest Expense, Including Capitalized Interest}}$

| | |
|---|---|
| Net sales | $2,400,000 |
| Cost of sales | (1,600,000) |
| Selling and administrative expenses | (200,000) |
| Earnings before interest and tax | $ 600,000 |

$$\frac{\text{Earnings before interest and tax}}{\text{Interest expense}} \quad \frac{\$\ 600,000}{\$\ \ 60,000} = 10.0$$

d 19.

| | |
|---|---|
| Earnings before interest and tax | $ 600,000 |
| Plus depreciation | 200,000 |
| Adjusted earnings before interest and tax | $ 800,000 |

$$\frac{\text{Adjusted Earnings Before Interest And Tax}}{\text{Interest Expense}} \quad \frac{\$\ 800,000}{\$\ \ 60,000} = 13.3$$

d 20. $\dfrac{\text{Recurring Earnings, Excluding Interest Expense, Tax Expense, Equity Earnings, and Minority Earnings}}{\text{Interest Expense, Including Capitalized Interest}}$

| | |
|---|---|
| Net sales | $1,800,000 |
| Cost of sales | (1,400,000) |
| Selling and administrative expenses | ( 250,000) |
| Earnings before interest and tax | $ 150,000 |

$$\frac{\text{Earnings before interest and tax}}{\text{Interest Expense}} \quad \frac{\$150,000}{\$\ 50,000} = 3.0$$

<u>  d  </u> 21. Recurring Earnings, Excluding Interest Expense,
Tax Expense, Equity Earnings, and Minority Income
<u>+ Interest Portion of Rentals</u>
Interest Expense, Including Capitalized Interest
+ Interest Portion of Rentals

| | |
|---|---:|
| Net sales | $1,800,000 |
| Cost of sales | (1,400,000) |
| Selling and administrative expenses | ( 250,000) |
| Earnings before interest and tax | 150,000 |
| Plus 1/3 of operating lease<br>  payments ($30,000 x 1/3) | 10,000 |
| Adjusted earnings before interest and tax | $ 160,000 |
| | |
| Interest expense | $ 50,000 |
| 1/3 of operating lease payments | 10,000 |
| Fixed charges | $ 60,000 |

$$\text{Fixed Charge Coverage} = \frac{\$160,000}{\$60,000} = 2.67$$

<u>  c  </u> 22. <u>Total Liabilities</u>
Total Assets

| | |
|---|---:|
| Total liabilities and shareholders' equity | $365,000 |
| Less: Shareholders' equity | 160,000 |
| Total liabilities | $205,000 |
| | |
| Total liabilities | $205,000 = .56 |
| Total liabilities and shareholders' equity | $365,000 |

<u>  b  </u> 23. <u>  Total Liabilities  </u>
Shareholders' Equity

| | |
|---|---:|
| Total liabilities and shareholders' equity | $365,000 |
| Less: Shareholders' equity | 160,000 |
| Total liabilities | $205,000 |
| | |
| Total Liabilities | $205,000 = 1.28 |
| Shareholders' Equity | $160,000 |

<u>  c  </u> 24. <u>              Total Liabilities          </u>
Shareholders' Equity - Intangible Assets

| | |
|---|---:|
| Total liabilities and shareholders' equity | $365,000 |
| Less: Shareholders' equity | 160,000 |
| Total liabilities | $205,000 |

$$\frac{\$205,000}{\$160,000 - 40,000} = 1.71$$

Chapter 7 - Problem 3 - True/False

| | | | | | | |
|---|---|---|---|---|---|
| T | 1. | F | 12. | F | 23. |
| F | 2. | T | 13. | F | 24. |
| F | 3. | F | 14. | T | 25. |
| T | 4. | F | 15. | F | 26. |
| F | 5. | F | 16. | T | 27. |
| T | 6. | F | 17. | T | 28. |
| T | 7. | F | 18. | F | 29. |
| F | 8. | F | 19. | F | 30. |
| T | 9. | F | 20. | T | 31. |
| T | 10. | F | 21. | T | 32. |
| T | 11. | F | 22. | T | 33. |

Chapter 7 - Problem 4 - Matching Computation of Ratios

| | |
|---|---|
| e | 1. |
| c | 2. |
| a | 3. |
| b | 4. |
| d | 5. |

Chapter 7 - Problem 5 - Matching Pension Plan Terms

| | | | |
|---|---|---|---|
| a | 1. | f | 6. |
| c | 2. | i | 7. |
| d | 3. | h | 8. |
| g | 4. | b | 9. |
| e | 5. | | |

Chapter 8 - Problem 6 - Compute the Times Interest Earned And Fixed Charge Coverage

a.    Times Interest Earned = $\dfrac{\text{Recurring Earnings Before Interest Expense, Tax Minority Income, and Equity Interest}}{\text{Interest Expense, Including Capitalized Interest}}$

| | | |
|---|---|---|
| Income before income taxes | $18,000 | |
| Plus interest | 1,000 | |
| Adjusted income | $19,000 | (A) |
| Interest expense | $ 1,000 | (B) |

Times Interest Earned = $\dfrac{\text{(A) } \$19,000}{\text{(B) } \$1,000}$ = 19 times

b.  Fixed charge coverage = $\dfrac{\begin{array}{c}\text{Recurring Earnings Before Interest} \\ \text{Expense, Tax, Minority Income,} \\ \text{and Equity Earnings +} \\ \text{Interest Portion of Rentals}\end{array}}{\begin{array}{c}\text{Interest Expense, Including} \\ \text{Capitalized Interest + Interest} \\ \text{Portion of Rentals}\end{array}}$

| | |
|---|---:|
| Income before income taxes | $18,000 |
| Plus interest | 1,000 |
| Adjusted income | 19,000 |
| 1/3 of operating lease payments | 200 |
| | $19,200 (A) |

| | | |
|---|---:|---|
| Interest expense | $1,000 | |
| 1/3 of operating lease payments | 200 | |
| | $1,200 | (B) |

Fixed Charge Coverage = $\dfrac{\text{(A) } \$19,200}{\text{(B) } \$1,200}$ = 16 times

Chapter 7 - Problem 7 - Computation of Debt Ratios

a.  Times Interest Earned =

| | | |
|---|---|---:|
| Net sales | | $32,000 |
| Less cost of goods sold | | (24,000) |
| Selling and administrative expenses | | ( 3,600) |
| | (A) | $ 4,400 |

| | | |
|---|---|---:|
| Interest expense | | $   180 |
| Capitalized interest | | 100 |
| Total interest | (B) | $   280 |

| | | |
|---|---|---|
| | (A)/(B) | 15.7 Times |

b. Fixed Charge = $\dfrac{\begin{array}{c}\text{Recurring Earnings Before}\\ \text{Interest Expense, Tax, Minority}\\ \text{Earnings, Equity Earnings, Plus}\\ \text{Interest Portion of Rentals}\end{array}}{\begin{array}{c}\text{Interest Expense Including}\\ \text{Capitalized Interest Plus}\\ \text{Interest Portion of Rentals}\end{array}}$

| | | |
|---|---|---|
| From part (a) | | $4,400 |
| Interest portion of rentals | | 600 |
| | (A) | $5,000 |

| | | |
|---|---|---|
| From part (a) | | $ 280 |
| Interest portion of rentals | | 600 |
| | (B) | $ 880 |

(A)/(B)   5.68 Times

c. Debt Ratio = $\dfrac{\text{Total Liabilities}}{\text{Total Assets}}$

$$\frac{\$1,000 + \$400 + \$1,900}{\$10,100} = \frac{\$3,300}{\$10,100} = 32.7\%$$

d. Debt/Equity Ratio = $\dfrac{\text{Total Liabilities}}{\text{Stockholders' Equity}}$

$$\frac{\$1,000 + \$400 + \$1,900}{\$6,800} = \frac{\$3,300}{\$6,800} = 48.5\%$$

e. $\dfrac{\text{Debt to Tangible}}{\text{Net Worth}} = \dfrac{\text{Total Liabilities}}{\text{Stockholders' Equity - Intangibles}}$

$$\frac{\$1,000 + \$400 + \$1,900}{\$6,800 - \$300} = \frac{\$3,300}{\$6,500} = 50.8\%$$

# Chapter 8: Profitability

<u>Chapter 8 - Problem 1 - Supply the Words Necessary to</u>
<u>Complete the Following Items</u>

1.  In analyzing profit, _____ figures are less meaningful than earnings measured in terms _____ to a number of bases.

2.  In general, the primary financial analysis of profit ratios should include only _____ that is expected to occur in _____ _____.

3.  A commonly used profit measure is return on sales, often termed ____ _____ _____.

4.  Equity income distorts the net profit margin on the _____ _____.

5.  Total asset turnover measures the activity of the _____ and the ability of the firm to generate _____ through the use of the assets.

6.  Return on assets measures the firm's ability to utilize its _____ to create _____.

7.  The rate of return on assets can be broken down into two component ratios, the ____ _____ _____ and _____ _____ _____.

8.  Operating income is net sales less ____ __ _____ and _____ _____.

9.  Operating assets exclude _____, _____, and the other assets category from total assets.

10. The DuPont analysis, considering only operating accounts, requires a computation of operating income and _____ _____.

11. The operating asset turnover measures the firm's ability to make productive use of its property, plant, and equipment by generating _____ _____.

12. Return on investment is a broad term applied to ratios measuring the relationship between the income earned and the _____ _____.

13. Preferred stock subject to mandatory redemption is termed _____ _____ stock.

14. Return on common equity measures return to the _____ shareholder.

15. _____ ___ _____ measures return to all providers of funds, since total assets equal total liabilities and equity.

16. Gross profit is the difference between net sales revenue and the _____ ___ _____ _____.

17. Interim reports contain more _____ in the financial data than in the _____ _____.

## Chapter 8 - Problem 2 - Multiple Choice

Choose the best answer for each of the following questions and enter the identifying letter in the space provided.

_____ 1. Which of the following is **not** considered to be a nonrecurring item?

    a. discontinued operations
    b. extraordinary items
    c. cumulative effect of change in accounting principle
    d. interest expense
    e. none of the above

_____ 2. Ideally, which of these ratios will indicate the highest return for an individual firm?

    a. return on assets
    b. return on assets variation
    c. return on investments
    d. return on total equity
    e. return on common equity

_____ 3. If a firm's gross profit has declined substantially, this could be attributed to all but one of the following reasons:

   a. The cost of buying inventory has increased more rapidly than selling prices.
   b. Selling prices have declined due to competition.
   c. Selling prices have increased due to competition.
   d. The mix of goods has changed to include more products with lower margins.
   e. Theft is occurring.

_____ 4. Gross profit analysis could be of value for all but one of the following:

   a. projections of profitability
   b. estimating administrative expenses
   c. inventory for interim statements
   d. estimating inventory for insurance claims
   e. replacing the physical taking of inventory on an annual basis

_____ 5. Total asset turnover measures:

   a. net income dollars generated by each dollar of sales.
   b. the ability of the firm to generate sales through the use of the assets.
   c. the firm's ability to make productive use of its property, plant, and equipment through generation of profits.
   d. the relationship between the income earned on the capital invested.
   e. return to the common shareholders.

_____ 6. Equity earnings can represent a problem in analyzing profitability because:

   a. equity earnings may not be related to cash flow.
   b. equity earnings are extraordinary.
   c. equity earnings are unusual.
   d. equity earnings are not from operations.
   e. equity earnings are equal to dividends received.

_____ 7. Which of the following is **not** a type of operating asset?

   a. intangibles
   b. receivables
   c. land
   d. inventory
   e. building

_____ 8. Earnings based on percent of holdings by outside owners of consolidated subsidiaries are termed:

   a. equity earnings.
   b. earnings of subsidiaries.
   c. investment income.
   d. minority earnings.
   e. none of the above.

_____ 9. Net profit margin x total asset turnover measures:

   a. DuPont return on assets
   b. Return on investment
   c. Return on stockholders' equity
   d. Return on common equity
   e. None of the above

_____ 10. Return on assets cannot rise under which of the following circumstances:

|   | Net profit margin | Total asset turnover |
|---|---|---|
| a. | decline | rise |
| b. | rise | decline |
| c. | rise | rise |
| d. | decline | decline |
| e. | The ratio could rise under all of the above. | |

_____ 11. A reason that equity earnings create a problem in analyzing profitability is because:

   a. equity earnings are non-recurring.
   b. equity earnings are extraordinary.
   c. equity earnings are usually less than the related cash flow.
   d. equity earnings relate to operations.
   e. none of the above.

_____ 12. Which of the following ratios will usually have the highest percent?

a. return on investment
b. return on total equity
c. return on common equity
d. return on total assets
e. there is not enough information to tell

_____ 13. Which of the following ratios will usually have the lowest percent?

a. return on investment
b. return on total equity
c. return on common equity
d. return on total assets
e. there is not enough information to tell

_____ 14. Which of the following items will be reported on the income statement as part of net income?

a. prior period adjustment
b. unrealized decline in market value of investments
c. foreign currency translation
d. gain from selling land
e. none of the above

_____ 15. Minority share of earnings is:

a. the total earnings of unconsolidated subsidiaries.
b. earnings based on the percent of holdings by the parent of unconsolidated subsidiaries.
c. total earnings of unconsolidated subsidiaries.
d. earnings based on the percent of holdings by outside owners of nonconsolidated subsidiaries.
e. none of the above.

_____ 16. Which of the following could cause return on assets to decline when net profit margin is increasing?

a. purchase of land at year-end
b. increase in book value
c. a stock dividend
d. increased turnover of operating assets
e. none of the above

Questions 17-29 are based on the following information:

Colleen Dandar Company presented the following income statement in its 2002 annual report:

| (Dollars in thousands except per share amounts) | 2002 | 2001 | 2000 |
|---|---|---|---|
| Net sales | $460,000 | $430,000 | $420,000 |
| Cost of sales | 276,000 | 262,300 | 248,000 |
| Gross profit | 184,000 | 167,700 | 172,000 |
| Selling, administrative, and other expenses | 115,000 | 106,000 | 101,000 |
| Operating earnings | 69,000 | 61,700 | 71,000 |
| Interest expense | 7,000 | 6,900 | 6,800 |
| Earnings before income taxes, and minority interest | 62,000 | 54,800 | 64,200 |
| Income taxes | (18,600) | (16,200) | (19,300) |
| Minority interests | ( 1,000) | ( 900) | ( 850) |
| Net earnings | $ 42,400 | $ 37,700 | $ 44,050 |
| Basic earnings per share | $3.20 | $2.85 | $3.32 |

The balance sheet for Colleen Dandar Company for 2000, 2001, and 2002 is summarized as follows:

| (in thousands) | 2002 | 2001 | 2000 |
|---|---|---|---|
| Assets: | | | |
| Current assets | $140,000 | $130,000 | $127,000 |
| Property, plant, and equipment, net | 250,000 | 248,000 | 246,000 |
| Other assets | 9,500 | 11,000 | 11,500 |
| Total assets | $399,500 | $389,000 | $384,500 |
| | | | |
| Liabilities and shareholders' equity: | | | |
| Liabilities: | | | |
| Current liabilities | $ 70,000 | $ 65,000 | $ 60,000 |
| Long-term liabilities | 150,000 | 160,000 | 162,000 |
| Total liabilities | $220,000 | $225,000 | $222,000 |
| | | | |
| Shareholders' equity: | | | |
| Preferred stock | $ 40,000 | $ 40,000 | $ 40,000 |
| Common stock | 75,000 | 75,000 | 75,000 |
| Retained earnings | 64,500 | 49,000 | 47,500 |
| Shareholders' equity | 179,500 | 164,000 | 162,500 |
| Total liabilities and shareholders' equity | $ 399,500 | $389,000 | $384,500 |

Note: Preferred dividends in each year are $3,200.

(Use ending balance sheet figures for your computations.)

_____ 17.    The Net Profit Margin for 2002, 2001, and 2000 is:

    a.    9.43%,    8.98%,  10.69%
    b.    9.43%,  10.84%,  10.69%
    c.    9.43%,  10.84%,  11.00%
    d.  10.86%,    9.92%,  11.68%
    e.  none of the above

_____ 18.    The Total Asset Turnover for 2002, 2001, and 2000 is:

    a.  10.86,    9.92,  11.68
    b.    2.31    2.28,    2.28
    c.    9.43,  10.84,  10.69
    d.    1.15,    1.11,    1.09
    e.  none of the above

_____ 19.   The Return On Assets for 2002, 2001, and 2000 is:

    a.  10.86%,   9.92%,  11.68%
    b.   9.43%,   8.98%,  10.69%
    c.  10.84%,   9.97%,  11.65%
    d.   1.18%,   1.14%,   1.13%
    e.  none of the above


_____ 20.   The DuPont Return on Assets for 2002, 2001, and 2000
            is:

    a.  23.62%,  22.99%,  27.11%
    b.  10.84%,   9.97%,  11.65%
    c.  15.00%,  14.35%,  16.90%
    d.  14.66%,  13.41%,  15.30%
    e.  none of the above


_____ 21.   The Operating Income Margin for 2002, 2001, and 2000
            is:

    a.  17.70%,  16.36%,  19.10%
    b.  10.84%,   9.97%,  11.65%
    c.  10.84%,   9.97%,  11.65%
    d.  15.00%,  14.35%,  16.90%
    e.  none of the above


_____ 22.   The Operating Asset Turnover for 2002, 2001, and
            2000 is:

    a.  1.18,  1.14,  1.13
    b.  1.84,  1.73,  1.71
    c.  1.15,  1.11,  1.09
    d.  1.18,  1.14,  1.20
    e.  none of the above


_____ 23.   The Return on Operating Assets for 2002, 2001, and
            2000 is:

    a.   9.43%,   8.98%,  10.69%
    b.  17.69%,  16.32%,  19.03%
    c.  17.70%,  16.36%,  19.10%
    d.  14.66%,  13.41%,  15.30%
    e.  none of the above

_____ 24.  The DuPont Return on Operating Assets for 2002,
            2001, and 2000 is:

            a.  10.86%,   9.92%,  11.68%
            b.   9.43%,   8.98%,  10.69%
            c.  17.70%,  16.36%,  19.10%
            d.  14.66%,  13.41%,  15.30%
            e.  none of the above

_____ 25.  The Sales To Fixed Assets for 2002, 2001, and 2000
            is:

            a.  2.18,  2.14,  2.13
            b.  1.18,  1.14,  1.13
            c.  1.15,  1.11,  1.09
            d.  1.84,  1.73,  1.71
            e.  none of the above

_____ 26.  The Return On Investment for 2002, 2001, and 2000
            is:

            a.  10.86%,   9.92%,  11.68%
            b.   9.43%,   8.98%,  10.69%
            c.  14.66%,  13.41%,  15.30%
            d.  23.62%,  22.99%,  27.11%
            e.  none of the above

_____ 27.  The Return On Total Equity for 2002, 2001, and 2000
            is:

            a.  23.62%,  22.99%,  27.11%
            b.   9.43%,  10.84%,  11.00%
            c.  10.86%,   9.92%,  11.68%
            d.  15.00%,  14.35%,  16.90%
            e.  none of the above

_____ 28.  The Return On Common Equity for 2002, 2001, and 2000
            is:

            a.  10.86%,   9.92%,  11.68%
            b.   9.43%,   8.98%,  10.69%
            c.  23.62%,  22.99%,  27.11%
            d.  28.10%,  27.82%,  33.35%
            e.  none of the above

_____ 29.    The Gross Profit Margin for 2002, 2001, and 2000 is:

a.  40.00%, 39.00%, 40.95%
b.  10.86%,  9.92%, 11.68%
c.  23.62%, 22.99%, 27.11%
d.  28.10%, 27.82%, 33.35%
e.  none of the above


Chapter 8 - Problem 3 - True/False

Indicate whether each of the following is true (T) or false (F) in the space provided.

_____ 1.    In general, trend analysis should consider only income that is expected to occur in subsequent periods.

_____ 2.    The net profit margin, the total asset turnover and return on assets are usually reviewed together because of the direct influence that the net profit margin and the total asset turnover have on return on assets.

_____ 3.    Equity earnings are always greater than the cash flow generated from the investment during a particular period of time.

_____ 4.    Technically, the net profit margin should exclude equity earnings and net other income.

_____ 5.    The operating ratios may give significantly different results from net earnings ratios if a firm has large amounts of nonoperating assets.

_____ 6.    The sales to fixed assets ratio will probably be substantially lower if the firm has relatively new fixed assets or if the firm is labor intensive.

_____ 7.    Return on investment measures return to only long-term suppliers of funds and is usually lower than return on assets.

_____ 8.    Ideally, the rate of return on equity ratios will be higher than the return on investment.

_____ 9.    Return on assets measures the firm's ability to utilize its assets to create profits.

_____ 10.   The rate of return on assets can be broken into two component ratios, the net profit margin and total inventory turnover.

_____ 11. Equity earnings can distort the profit margin.

_____ 12. On a balance sheet, redeemable preferred stock is categorized separately and not combined with other equity securities.

_____ 13. Preferred dividends are deducted on the income statement to arrive at net income.

_____ 14. One might expect common shareholders to earn the highest return, since they take the greatest degree of risk.

_____ 15. The income tax expense is an example of a figure that can require considerable judgment and estimation for an interim report.

_____ 16. In profitability analysis, absolute numbers and relative numbers can both be meaningful.

_____ 17. An increase in net profit margin can cause return on assets to fall.

_____ 18. Return on investment will typically be higher than return on equity.

_____ 19. Redeemable preferred stock is best considered as debt for ratio analysis.

_____ 20. Interim financial statements are usually more accurate than annual financial statements.

_____ 21. Interim reporting requires estimation of some expense items.

_____ 22. For segment reporting the focus is on financial information that an enterprises decision makers use to make decisions about the enterprise's operating matters.

_____ 23. A stock dividend reduces total stockholders' equity.

_____ 24. A cash dividend declared and paid reduces net profit.

_____ 25. Treasury stock sold above cost increases total stockholders' equity.

_____ 26. Bonds converted into common stock reduces total stockholders' equity.

_____ 27.    Common stock sold for cash increases retained
               earnings.


Chapter 8 - Problem 4 - Matching

Listed below are several ratios.    Match the letter that goes with
each formula.

a.    net profit margin
b.    total asset turnover
c.    return on assets
d.    DuPont return on assets
e.    operating income margin
f.    operating asset turnover
g.    return on operating assets
h.    DuPont return on operating assets
i.    sales to fixed assets
j.    return on investment
k.    return on total equity
l.    return on common equity
m.    gross profit margin


_____ 1.    $$\frac{\text{Net Income before Nonrecurring Items - Preferred Dividends}}{\text{Average Common Equity}}$$

_____ 2.    $$\frac{\text{Net Income before Minority Share of Earnings and Nonrecurring Items} + [(\text{Interest Expense}) \times (1 - \text{Tax Rate})]}{\text{Average Long - Term Liabilities + Equity}}$$

_____ 3.    $$\frac{\text{Net Income before Minority Share of Earnings and Nonrecurring Items}}{\text{Net Sales}}$$

_____ 4.    $$\frac{\text{Net Income before Minority Share of Earnings and Nonrecurring Items}}{\text{Average Total Assets}}$$

_____ 5.    $$\frac{\text{Operating Income}}{\text{Net Sales}}$$

_____ 6.    $$\frac{\text{Operating Income}}{\text{Average Operating Assets}}$$

_____ 7.    $$\frac{\text{Net Sales}}{\text{Average Net Fixed Assets}}$$

_____ 8. $$\frac{\text{Net Income before Nonrecurring Items -}}{\text{Average Total Equity}}$$

_____ 9. $$\frac{\text{Gross Profit}}{\text{Net Sales}}$$

_____ 10. Operating Income Margin x Operating Asset Turnover

_____ 11. $$\frac{\text{Net Sales}}{\text{Average Operating Assets}}$$

_____ 12. Net Profit Margin x Total Asset Turnover

_____ 13. $$\frac{\text{Net Sales}}{\text{Average Total Assets}}$$

# Chapter 8 - Problem 5 - Computation of Ratios

The following are extracted from the financial statements of Jackie Inc. for 2002, and 2001:

|  | 2002 | 2001 |
|---|---|---|
| Net sales | $380,000 | $360,000 |
| Cost of sales | (192,000) | 186,000) |
| Selling and administrative expenses | ( 67,000) | ( 65,400) |
| Other income (expense) |  |  |
|   Interest | (4,000) | ( 3,800) |
|   Other | 400 | 600 |
| Earnings before tax and extra-ordinary credit | 117,400 | 105,400 |
| Provision for income tax | 42,000 | 40,000) |
| Earnings before extraordinary gain | 75,400 | 65,400 |
| Extraordinary gain (net of tax) | 6,000 |  |
| Net income | $ 81,400 | $ 65,400 |
|  |  |  |
| Total assets | $400,000 | $380,000 |
|  |  |  |
| Long-term debt | $160,000 | $162,000 |
| Common equity | $160,000 | $155,000 |
| Preferred stock | $ 20,000 | $ 20,000 |
| Preferred dividends | $ 800 | $ 800 |

**Required:** Compute the following ratios for 2002:
- a.  net profit margin
- b.  total asset turnover
- c.  return on assets
- d.  return on investment
- e.  return on total equity
- f.  return on common equity
- g.  gross profit margin
- h.  DuPont return on assets

# Chapter 8 - Problem 6 - Computation of Ratios

Data for Ernie's Auto Parts for 2002 is presented as follows:

## Income Statement Data

| | |
|---|---:|
| Net sales | $1,200,000 |
| Cost of goods sold | (880,000) |
| Gross profit | 320,000 |
| Operating expense | (110,000) |
| Operating income | 210,000 |
| Other expense (interest) | ( 10,000) |
| Earnings before income tax | 200,000 |
| Income taxes | ( 80,000) |
| Net income | 120,000 |
| Dividends paid | ( 20,000) |
| Net increase in retained earnings | $ 100,000 |

## Balance Sheet Data

### Assets

| | |
|---|---:|
| Cash | $ 25,000 |
| Receivables (net) | 110,000 |
| Inventory | 130,000 |
| Land, buildings, and equipment, net | 390,000 |
| Intangible assets | 15,000 |
| | $ 670,000 |

### Liabilities and Stockholders' Equity

| | |
|---|---:|
| Trade notes and accounts payable | $ 75,000 |
| Miscellaneous current liabilities | 20,000 |
| 8% Bonds payable | 250,000 |
| Common stock $5 par | 100,000 |
| Additional paid-in capital | 50,000 |
| Retained earnings | 175,000 |
| | $ 670,000 |

The market price at the end of the year was $50.

**Required:** Compute the following ratios:
   a.   net profit margin
   b.   total asset turnover (use year-end assets)
   c.   return on assets (use year-end assets)
   d.   operating income margin
   e.   operating asset turnover (use year-end assets)
   f.   return on operating assets (use year-end assets)

# Chapter 8 - Problem 7 - Vertical Common-Size Income Statement

Income statement data for White Corporation follows:

|                    | 2002        | 2001        |
|--------------------|-------------|-------------|
| Sales              | $2,600,000  | $2,000,000  |
| Cost of goods sold | 1,400,000   | 1,200,000   |
| Selling expense    | 270,000     | 230,000     |
| General expense    | 130,000     | 120,000     |
| Income tax expense | 280,000     | 220,000     |

**Required:**  a.  Prepare an income statement in comparative form, stating each item for both years as a percent of sales.

              b.  Comment on the findings in (a).

Chapter 8 - Problem 1 - Supply the Words Necessary to Complete the Following Items

1.  absolute, relative

2.  income, subsequent periods

3.  net profit margin

4.  high side

5.  assets; sales

6.  assets; profits

7.  net profit margin; total asset turnover

8.  cost of sales; operating expenses

9.  investments, intangibles

10.  operating assets

11.  sales dollars

12.  capital invested

13.  redeemable preferred

14.  common

15.  Return on assets

16.  cost of goods sold

17.  estimates; annual reports


Chapter 8 - Problem 2 - Multiple Choice

  d    1.   Interest expense represents a recurring item.

  e    2.   Ideally, return on common equity will indicate the highest return.  This is the way it should be, since the common equityholders take the most risk.

  c    3.   A selling price increase would increase the gross profit.

b    4. It would not be feasible to estimate administrative expenses by using gross profit analysis.

b    5. Total asset turnover measures the ability of the firm to generate sales through the use of assets.

d    6. Equity earnings can represent a problem in analyzing profitability because equity earnings are not from operations.

a    7. Intangibles are not considered to be an operating asset.

d    8. Earnings based on percent of holdings by outside owners of consolidated subsidiaries are termed minority earnings.

a    9. Net profit margin x total asset turnover measures DuPont return on assets.

d   10. If net profit margin declines and the total asset turnover declines, then the return on assets cannot rise.

c   11. A reason that equity earnings create a problem in analyzing profitability is because equity earnings are usually less than the related cash flow.

c   12. Usually the return on common equity will have the highest percent of the ratios listed.

d   13. Usually the return on total assets will have the lowest percent of the ratios listed.

d   14. Gain from selling land will be reported on the income statement.

e   15. None of the above describes minority share of earnings.

a   16. Purchase of land at year-end could cause return on assets to decline when the net profit margin is increasing. The year-end purchase of land would not have contributed to profits.

<u>a</u>  17. Net Income Before Minority Share of Earnings and
<u>Nonrecurring Items</u>
Net Sales

| | 2002 | 2001 | 2000 |
|---|---|---|---|
| Net earnings | $ 42,400 | $ 37,700 | $ 44,050 |
| Plus minority interest | 1,000 | 900 | 850 |
| | $ 43,400 | $ 38,600 | $ 44,900 |
| Net sales | $460,000 | $430,000 | $420,000 |
| Net Profit Margin | 9.43% | 8.98% | 10.69% |

<u>d</u>  18. <u>Net Sales</u>
Average Total Assets

| | 2002 | 2001 | 2000 |
|---|---|---|---|
| Net sales | $460,000 | $430,000 | $420,000 |
| Total assets | $399,500 | $389,000 | $384,500 |
| Total Asset Turnover | 1.15 | 1.11 | 1.09 |

<u>a</u>  19. Net Income Before Minority Share of
<u>Earnings and Nonrecurring Items</u>
Average Total Assets

| | 2002 | 2001 | 2000 |
|---|---|---|---|
| Net earnings | $ 42,400 | $ 37,700 | $ 44,050 |
| Plus minority interests | 1,000 | 900 | 850 |
| | $ 43,400 | $ 38,600 | $ 44,900 |
| Total assets | $399,500 | $389,000 | $384,500 |
| Return On Assets | 10.86% | 9.92% | 11.68% |

<u>b</u>  20. DuPont Return On Assets = Net Profit Margin
x Total Asset Turnover

| | 2002 | 2001 | 2000 |
|---|---|---|---|
| Net profit margin | 9.43% | 8.98% | 10.69% |
| Total asset turnover | x1.15 | x1.11 | x1.09 |
| DuPont Return on Assets | 10.84% | 9.97% | 11.65% |

<u>d</u>  21. <u>Operating Income</u>
Net Sales

| | 2002 | 2001 | 2000 |
|---|---|---|---|
| Operating income | $ 69,000 | $ 61,700 | $ 71,000 |
| Net sales | $460,000 | $430,000 | $420,000 |
| Operating Income Margin | 15.00% | 14.35% | 16.90% |

## a  22.  Net Sales / Average Operating Assets

|  | 2002 | 2001 | 2000 |
|---|---|---|---|
| Net sales | $460,000 | $430,000 | $420,000 |
| Operating assets: | | | |
| Total assets | $399,500 | $389,000 | $384,500 |
| Less other | ( 9,500) | (11,000) | (11,500) |
|  | $390,000 | $378,000 | $373,000 |
| Operating Asset Turnover | 1.18 | 1.14 | 1.13 |

## b  23.  Operating Income / Average Operating Assets

|  | 2002 | 2001 | 2000 |
|---|---|---|---|
| Operating income | $ 69,000 | $ 61,700 | $ 71,000 |
| Operating assets | $390,000 | $378,000 | $373,000 |
| Return On Operating Assets | 17.69% | 16.32% | 19.03% |

## c  24.  Operating Income Margin x Operating Asset Turnover

|  | 2002 | 2001 | 2000 |
|---|---|---|---|
| Operating income margin | 15.00% | 14.35% | 16.90% |
| (Times) | | | |
| Operating asset turnover | 1.18 | 1.14 | 1.13 |
| DuPont return on operating assets | 17.70% | 16.36% | 19.10% |

## d  25.  Net Sales / Average Net Fixed Assets

|  | 2002 | 2001 | 2000 |
|---|---|---|---|
| Net sales | $460,000 | $430,000 | $420,000 |
| Net fixed assets | $250,000 | $248,000 | $246,000 |
| Sales To Fixed Assets | 1.84 | 1.73 | 1.71 |

## c  26.  Net Income Before Minority Share of Earnings and Nonrecurring Items + (Interest Expense) x (1-Tax Rate) / Average (Long-term Liabilities & Equity)

|  | 2002 | 2001 | 2000 |
|---|---|---|---|
| Net earnings | $42,400 | $37,700 | $44,050 |
| Plus minority interest | 1,000 | 900 | 850 |
|  | 43,400 | 38,600 | 44,900 |
| Plus: (Interest Expense x (1 - tax rate) | | | |
| (7,000) x (1-.030) | 4,900 | | |
| (6,900) x (1-.296) | | 4,858 | |
| (6,800) x (1-.301) | | | 4,753 |
|  | $ 48,300 | $ 43,458 | $ 49,653 |
| Long-term liabilities + equity | $329,500 | $324,000 | $324,500 |
|  | 14.66% | 13.41% | 15.30% |

__a__ 27. Net Income Before Nonrecurring Items -
Dividends on Redeemable Preferred Stock
Average Total Equity

|  | 2002 | 2001 | 2000 |
|---|---|---|---|
| Net income | $ 42,400 | $ 37,700 | $ 44,050 |
| Total equity | $179,500 | $164,000 | $162,500 |
|  | 23.62% | 22.99% | 27.11% |

__d__ 28. Net Income Before Nonrecurring Items -
Preferred Dividends
Average Common Equity

|  | 2002 | 2001 | 2000 |
|---|---|---|---|
| Net income | $ 42,400 | $ 37,700 | $ 44,050 |
| Less: Preferred dividends | 3,200 | 3,200 | 3,200 |
|  | $ 39,200 | $ 34,500 | $ 40,850 |
| Common equity: |  |  |  |
| Common stock | $ 75,000 | $ 75,000 | $ 75,000 |
| Retained earnings | 64,500 | 49,000 | 47,500 |
|  | $139,500 | $124,000 | $122,500 |
|  | 28.10% | 27.82% | 33.35% |

__a__ 29. Gross Profit
Net Sales

|  | 2002 | 2001 | 2000 |
|---|---|---|---|
| Gross profit | $184,000 | $167,700 | $172,000 |
| Net sales | $460,000 | $430,000 | $420,000 |
|  | 40.00% | 39.00% | 40.95% |

## Chapter 8 - Problem 3 - True/False

| | | | | | | | |
|---|---|---|---|---|---|---|---|
| __T__ | 1. | __F__ | 10. | __T__ | 19. |
| __T__ | 2. | __F__ | 11. | __F__ | 20. |
| __F__ | 3. | __T__ | 12. | __T__ | 21. |
| __T__ | 4. | __F__ | 13. | __T__ | 22. |
| __T__ | 5. | __T__ | 14. | __F__ | 23. |
| __T__ | 6. | __T__ | 15. | __F__ | 24. |
| __F__ | 7. | __T__ | 16. | __T__ | 25. |
| __T__ | 8. | __F__ | 17. | __F__ | 26. |
| __T__ | 9. | __F__ | 18. | __F__ | 27. |

# Chapter 8 - Problem 4 - Matching Ratio Computations

| | | | |
|---|---|---|---|
| l | 1. | k | 8. |
| j | 2. | m | 9. |
| a | 3. | h | 10. |
| c | 4. | f | 11. |
| e | 5. | d | 12. |
| g | 6. | b | 13. |
| i | 7. | | |

# Chapter 8 - Problem 5 - Computation of Ratios

a.    Net Profit Margin = $\dfrac{\text{Net Income Before Minority Share of Earnings and Nonrecurring Items}}{\text{Net Sales}}$

$$\frac{\$75,400}{\$380,000} = 19.84\%$$

b.    Total Asset Turnover = $\dfrac{\text{Net Sales}}{\text{Average Total Assets}}$

$$\frac{\$380,000}{(\$400,000 + \$380,000) / 2} = .97 \text{ Times}$$

c.    Return On Assets = $\dfrac{\text{Net Income Before Minority Share of Earnings and Nonrecurring Items}}{\text{Average Total Assets}}$

$$\frac{\$75,400}{(\$400,000 + \$380,000) / 2} = 19.33\%$$

d.    Return On Investment = $\dfrac{\text{Net Income Before Minority Share of Earnings and Nonrecurring Items} + (\text{Interest Expense}) * (1 - \text{Tax Rate})}{\text{Average (Long - Term Liabilities + Equity)}}$

Net income before extraordinary item          $ 75,400
Interest expense                               $  4,000
Tax rate:

$$\frac{\$42,000}{\$117,400} = 35.78\%$$

Interest expense * (1-tax rate)
($4,000 x 64.22%) = $2,569
Net income before extraordinary
  item + interest expense (1-tax rate)
  ($75,400 + $2,569)                           $ 77,969  (A)

Long-term liabilities and stockholders' equity:

Beginning of year:
  Long-term debt                               $162,000
  Common equity                                 155,000
  Preferred stock                                20,000

End of year:
  Long-term debt                                160,000
  Common equity                                 160,000
  Preferred stock                                20,000
Total                                          $677,000
Average          $677,000/2                     338,500  (B)


Return On Investment (A) / (B)         $\frac{\$77,969}{\$338,500} = 23.03\%$

e.   Return On Equity = $\dfrac{\text{Net Income Before Nonrecurring Items - Dividends on Redeemable Preferred Stock}}{\text{Average Total Equity}}$

Net income before non-recurring
  items - Dividends on redeemable
  preferred stock                              $ 75,400  (A)


Total equity:
Beginning of year:
  Common equity                                $155,000
  Preferred stock                                20,000
End of year:
  Common stock                                  160,000
  Preferred stock                                20,000
Total                                          $355,000
Average          $355,000/2                    $177,500  (B)


Return On Equity (A) / (B)   $\frac{\$75,400}{\$177,500} = 42.48\%$

191

f.　Return On Common Equity $= \dfrac{\text{Net Income Before Nonrecurring Items} - \text{Preferred Dividends}}{\text{Average Common Equity}}$

| | |
|---|---|
| Net income before non-recurring items | $ 75,400 |
| Less: Preferred dividends | (800) |
| Adjusted income | $ 74,600 (A) |

| | | |
|---|---|---|
| Total common equity: | | |
| Beginning of year | | $155,000 |
| End of year | | 160,000 |
| Total | | $315,000 |
| Average | $315,000/2 | $157,500 (B) |

Return On Common Equity (A)/(B)　$\dfrac{\$74,600}{\$157,500} = 47.37\%$

g.　Gross Profit Margin $= \dfrac{\text{Gross Profit}}{\text{Net Sales}}$

| | |
|---|---|
| Net sales | $380,000 (B) |
| Cost of sales | (192,000) |
| Gross profit | $188,000 (A) |

Gross Profit Margin (A)/(B)　$\dfrac{\$188,000}{\$380,000} = 49.47\%$

h.　DuPont Return On Assets

Return On Assets = Net Profit Margin x Total Asset Turnover

| 19.24% | = | 19.84% | x | .97 |
|---|---|---|---|---|

Chapter 8 - Problem 6 - Computation of Ratios

a.　Net Profit Margin $= \dfrac{\text{Net Income Before Minority Share of Earnings and Nonrecurring Items}}{\text{Net Sales}}$

$\dfrac{\$120,000}{\$1,200,000} = 10.00\%$

b.　Total Asset Turnover $= \dfrac{\text{Net Sales}}{\text{Total Assets}}$

$\dfrac{\$1,200,000}{\$670,000} = 1.79 \text{ Times}$

c. Return On Assets = $\dfrac{\text{Net Income Before Minority Share of Earnings and Nonrecurring Items}}{\text{Total Assets}}$

$$\dfrac{\$120,000}{\$670,000} = 17.91\%$$

d. Operating Income Margin = $\dfrac{\text{Operating Income}}{\text{Net Sales}}$

$$\dfrac{\$210,000}{\$1,200,000} = 17.50\%$$

e. Operating Asset Turnover = $\dfrac{\text{Net Sales}}{\text{Operating Assets}}$

$$\dfrac{\$1,200,000}{\$670,000 - \$15,000} = 1.83 \text{ Times}$$

f. Return On Operating Assets = $\dfrac{\text{Operating Income}}{\text{Operating Assets}}$

$$\dfrac{\$210,000}{\$670,000 - \$15,000} = 32.06\%$$

Chapter 8 - Problem 7 - Vertical Common-Size Income Statement

a.

|  | 2002 | 2001 |
|---|---|---|
| Sales | 100.0% | 100.0% |
| Cost of goods sold | 53.8 | 60.0 |
| Gross profit | 46.2 | 40.0 |
| Selling expense | 10.4 | 11.5 |
| General expense | 5.0 | 6.0 |
| Operating income | 30.8 | 22.5 |
| Income tax | 10.8 | 11.0 |
| Net income | 20.0 | 11.5 |

b. White Corporation had a dramatic increase in income because of improvements in all cost areas, especially cost of goods sold.

# Chapter 9:  For the Investor

Chapter 9 - Problem 1 - Supply the Words Necessary to Complete
the Following Items

1.  Financial leverage is successful if more can be _____ on
    the borrowed funds than is _____ to use the funds.

2.  If financial leverage is used, a rise in EBIT will cause an
    even greater rise in ____ _____.

3.  The use of financial leverage, termed _____ ___ ____
    _____, is successful only if the rate of earnings on
    borrowed funds is _____ than the fixed charges.

4.  In periods of relatively ____ interest rates or declining
    interest rates, financial leverage is looked on more
    favorably than in periods of _____ interest rates or
    increasing interest rates.

5.  Two things are important in looking at financial leverage as
    part of financial analysis.  First, how _____ is the degree
    of financial leverage?  Second, in your opinion, is the
    financial leverage going to work ____ the owners or _____
    the owners?

6.  Earnings per share is the amount of income earned on a share
    of _____ _____ during an accounting period.

7.  The earnings per common share computation uses only earnings
    available to _____ _____ in the numerator of the
    computation.

8.  Stock dividends and stock splits do _____ provide the firm
    with more _____; they only change the _____ of
    outstanding shares.

9.  The price/earnings ratio, commonly termed _____, expresses
    the relationship between the market price of a share of
    _____ _____ and that stock's current earnings per
    _____.

10. Ideally, the price/earnings ratio should be computed using
    _____ earnings per share after excluding _____
    earnings per share.

11. Price/earnings ratios do not have any meaning when a firm has abnormally ____ profits in relation to the asset base, or when a firm has _____.

12. Percentage of earnings retained measures the proportion of current earnings retained for _____ _____.

13. Dividend payout measures the portion of current earnings per common _____ that is being paid out in _____.

14. Dividend yield indicates the relationship between the _____ per common share and the _____ _____ per common share.

15. Book value is of _____ use to the investment analyst, since it is based on _____ costs.

16. With stock appreciation rights, the employee is given the right to receive compensation in _____ or _____ or a combination of these at some _____ date.

17. There are two types of stock option plans: one is a _____ plan and the other is a _____ plan.

18. Total earnings from securities include both _____ and price _____.


Chapter 9 - Problem 2 - Multiple Choice

Choose the best answer for each of the following questions and enter the identifying letter in the space provided.

_____ 1. In 2001 and 2002, Zoret Company reported earnings per share of 80¢ and $1.00, respectively. In 2003, Zoret Company declared a 4-for-1 stock split. For the year 2003, Zoret Company reported earnings of 30¢ per share. The appropriate earnings per share presentation for a 3-year comparative analysis that includes 2001, 2002, and 2003 would be:

|   | 2003 | 2002 | 2001 |
|---|------|------|------|
| a. | $ .30 | $ .25 | $ .80 |
| b. | $ .30 | $4.00 | $3.20 |
| c. | $ .30 | $ .25 | $ .20 |
| d. | $1.20 | $ .25 | $ .20 |
| e. | $1.20 | $4.00 | $3.20 |

_____ 2. MacKey Company reported the following for 2002:

| | |
|---|---|
| Ending market price | $40.00 |
| Earnings per share: | |
|   Basic | $ 2.50 |
|   Diluted | $ 2.00 |
| Dividends per share of common | $ 1.00 |
| Dividends per share of preferred | $ .50 |

The price earnings ratio and dividend payout were:

a. 20 and 25%
b. 16 and 25%
c. 20 and 20%
d. 20 and 50%
e. 16 and 50%

_____ 3. The following data pertain to Allen Company:

| | |
|---|---|
| Market price per share at year-end | $ 20.00 |
| Number of common shares | 5,000 |
| Number of preferred shares | 10,000 |
| Preferred stock | $100,000 |
| Common stock | $200,000 |
| Retained earnings | $250,000 |

The book value per share is:

a. $25
b. $50
c. $40
d. $10
e. $90

4. Radio Company had the following pattern of results related to stock appreciation rights:

| | |
|---|---:|
| Shares of stock outstanding | 100,000 |
| Shares in the plan | 10,000 |
| Option price | $ 20.00 |
| Market price - | |
| end of year 1 | $ 20.00 |
| end of year 2 | $ 30.00 |
| end of year 3 | $ 25.00 |

The compensation expense would be:

| | Year 1 | Year 2 | Year 3 |
|---|---|---|---|
| a. | $ 50,000 | $ 50,000 | $ 50,000 |
| b. | $ 50,000 | $100,000 | $ 50,000 |
| c. | -0- | $100,000 | $ 50,000 |
| d. | $100,000 | $ 50,000 | -0- |
| e. | -0- | $100,000 | <$ 50,000> |

5. The degree of financial leverage for the Zorro Company was 1.50 when EBIT was reported at $1,000,000. If EBIT goes to $2,000,000, the accompanying change in net income will be:

a. $2,500,000.
b. $3,000,000.
c. $2,000,000.
d. $1,500,000.
e. $1,000,000.

6. In 2003, Zello Company declared a 10% stock dividend. In 2002, earnings per share was $1.00. When the 2002 earnings per share is disclosed in the 2003 annual report, it will be disclosed at:

a. $1.00.
b. $1.10.
c. $1.20.
d. $ .91.
e. $ .81.

_____ 7. Which of the following ratios usually reflects investors opinions of the future prospects for the firm?

    a. Dividend yield
    b. Book value per share
    c. Price/earnings ratio
    d. Earnings per share
    e. Dividend payout

_____ 8. Which of the following ratios gives a perspective on risk in the capital structure?

    a. Book value per share
    b. Dividend yield
    c. Dividend payout
    d. Degree of financial leverage
    e. Price/earnings ratio

_____ 9. A summarized income statement for Abbet Company is presented below.

| | |
|---|---:|
| Sales | $800,000 |
| Cost of sales | (500,000) |
| Gross profit | 300,000 |
| Operating expenses | (100,000) |
| Operating income | 200,000 |
| Other income | 10,000 |
| Other expenses (including interest of $8,000) | ( 15,000) |
| Earnings before tax | 195,000 |
| Income tax | ( 80,000) |
| Net income | $115,000 |

The degree of financial leverage is:

    a. 1.05
    b. 1.18
    c. 1.08
    d. 1.28
    e. 1.04

_____ 10. The earnings per share ratio is computed for:

    a. convertible bonds.
    b. redeemable preferred.
    c. common stock.
    d. nonredeemable preferred.
    e. none of the above.

_____ 11. What is the immediate effect of granting stock options?

    a. It reduces profitability.
    b. Increases the number of shares outstanding.
    c. Creates the potential that those receiving the options may purchase the stock at a favorable price.
    d. Increases the number of shares outstanding and may dilute earnings per share.
    e. Generates cash for the firm.


_____ 12. Jacobs reported the following for 2002:

| | |
|---|---|
| Beginning market price | $26.00 |
| Average market price | $28.00 |
| Ending market price | $30.00 |
| Earnings per share: | |
|   Basic | $ 2.00 |
|   Diluted | $ 1.80 |
| Cash dividends per share | $ 1.20 |

The price earnings ratio and dividend payout were:

    a. 16.67 and 66.67%.
    b. 16.67 and 150.00%.
    c. 15.55 and 66.66%.
    d. 14.44 and 66.66%.
    e. none of the above.

_____ 13. The following data were gathered from the annual report of Arrow Care:

| | |
|---|---|
| Ending market price per share | $30.00 |
| Average market price per share | $26.00 |
| Number of common shares outstanding | 5,000 |
| Number of preferred shares | 1,000 |
| Preferred stock, $50 par | $10,000 |
| Common equity | $200,000 |

The book value per share is:

    a. $10.00.
    b. $35.00.
    c. $40.00.
    d. $42.00.
    e. none of the above.

_____ 14. Increasing financial leverage can be a risky strategy from the viewpoint of stockholders of companies having:

a. steady and high profits.
b. low and falling profits.
c. relative high and increasing profits.
d. a low debt/equity ratio and relatively high profits.
e. none of the above.

_____ 15. A firm has a degree of financial leverage of 1.3. If earnings before interest and tax increase by 10%, then net income:

a. will increase by 13.0%.
b. will increase by 13.
c. will decrease by 13.0%.
d. will decrease by 13.
e. none of the above.

_____ 16. This ratio represents dividends per common share in relation to market price per common share:

a. dividend payout
b. dividend yield
c. price/earnings
d. book value per share
e. percentage of earnings retained

_____ 17. Book value per share may **not** approximate market value per share because:

a. investments may have a market value substantially above the original cost.
b. land may have substantially increased in value.
c. market value reflects future potential earning power.
d. the firm owns patents that have substantial value.
e. all of the above.

Questions 18-19 are based on the following information:

The following data relate to Grover Company:

| | |
|---|---|
| Earnings per share: | |
| Basic | $ 1.00 |
| Diluted | .90 |
| Cash dividends per share (common) | .70 |
| Market price per common share | $15.00 |
| Total common dividends | $20,000 |
| Total preferred dividends | $ 5,000 |
| Net income | $40,000 |

_____ 18. The percentage of earnings retained is:

    a.  87.50%
    b.  50.00%
    c.  37.50%
    d.  40.00%
    e.  none of the above

_____ 19. The dividend yield is:

    a.   4.67%
    b.  37.50%
    c.  77.78%
    d.   6.67%
    e.  none of the above

Chapter 9 - Problem 3 - True/False

Indicate whether each of the following is true (T) or false (F) in the space provided.

_____ 1. Earnings per share is computed for both common stock and preferred stock.

_____ 2. Diluted earnings per share is a more conservative representation of earnings than is basic earnings per share.

_____ 3. A firm must pay preferred dividends each year.

_____ 4. Dividends are subtracted to calculate taxable income.

_____ 5. If financial leverage is used, a rise in earnings before interest and tax will cause an even greater rise in net income.

_____ 6. The degree of financial leverage will usually be constant for all levels of income.

_____ 7. The degree of financial leverage for Anet Company is 1.41 for 1998. This means that as earnings before interest changes in 1999, earnings to the common shareholder will change by 1.41 times that percent.

_____ 8. If used in the P/E ratio, diluted earnings per share will result in a lower price/earnings than if basic earnings per share was used in the P/E ratio.

_____ 9. Jones Company had earnings in 2000 of $6.00 per share. In 1999 earnings per share were $3.00 per share. Under these conditions, we would expect the price/earnings ratio to be high.

_____ 10. An increase in the market price per share will result in a lower dividend yield.

_____ 11. Book value per share indicates the amount of stockholders' equity that relates to each share of outstanding stock, preferred and common.

_____ 12. We would normally expect a company's stock to sell above book value.

_____ 13. Stock options outstanding usually decrease net income.

_____ 14. Stock options outstanding usually decrease earnings per share.

_____ 15. Stock options do not require a cash outlay from the company, while stock appreciation rights often do require a cash outlay.

_____ 16. In computing earnings per share, preferred dividends are added to net income.

_____ 17. Nonrecurring items, such as extraordinary income, should be removed from the income statement before computing earnings per share.

_____ 18. When a stock dividend occurs, earnings per share must be adjusted retrospectively.

_____ 19. Basic and diluted earnings per share are always part of the earnings per share presentation.

_____ 20. The lower the amount of interest expense, the lower the degree of financial leverage.

_____ 21. A firm might have a high dividend payout ratio if its opportunities for growth were bleak.

_____ 22. Dividend yield relates dividends per share to earnings per share.

_____ 23. Book value per share measures the book value of the net assets on a per share basis.

_____ 24. Market value will never go below book value.

_____ 25. The full impact of stock options is included in the earnings per share computation.

# Chapter 9 - Problem 4 - Matching Computation of Ratios

Listed below are several ratios. Match the letter that goes with each formula.

a. degree of financial leverage     e. dividend payout
b. basic earnings per common share     f. dividend yield
c. price/earnings ratio     g. book value per share
d. percentage of earnings retained

_____ 1.
$$\frac{\text{Total Stockholders' Equity - Preferred Stock Equity}}{\text{Number of Common Shares Outstanding}}$$

_____ 2.
$$\frac{\text{Dividends Per Common Share}}{\text{Diluted Earnings Per Share}}$$

_____ 3.
$$\frac{\text{Earnins Before Interest, Tax, Minority Share of Earnings, Equity Income, and Nonrecurring Items}}{\text{Earnings Before Tax, Minority Share of Earnings, Equity Income, and Nonrecurring Items}}$$

_____ 4.
$$\frac{\text{Net Income - Preferred Dividends}}{\text{Weighted Average Number of Common Shares Outstanding}}$$

_____ 5.
$$\frac{\text{Market Price Per Share}}{\text{Diluted Earnings Per Share}}$$

_____ 6.
$$\frac{\text{Net Income - All Dividends}}{\text{Net Income}}$$

_____ 7.
$$\frac{\text{Dividends Per Common Share}}{\text{Market Price Per Common Share}}$$

Chapter 9 - Problem 5 - Effect of a Transaction on a Given Ratio

Listed below in the left column is a specific ratio. In the
right column is a business transaction or situation. Indicate
the effect of this transaction on the given ratio. Use a + for
increase, - for decrease, and a 0 for no effect.

_____1. Percentage of earnings retained      Increased dividend payments

_____2. Degree of financial leverage         Bonds are issued

_____3. Price/earnings ratio                 Stock market price declines

_____4. Dividend payout                      Diluted earnings per
                                             share decreases

_____5. Dividend yield                       Stock market price increases

_____6. Book value per share                 The firm has profitable year

# Chapter 9 - Problem 6 - Computation of Ratios

Grogan Inc. reported the following balance sheet data in its 2001, December 31, year-end report to shareholders (presented in partial form):

| | |
|---|---:|
| Preferred stock, 7%, $100 par | $ 60,000 |
| Common stock, $10 par, 40,000 shares issued and outstanding | 400,000 |
| Paid-in capital in excess of par | 200,000 |
| Retained earnings | 220,000 |

In 2002, the firm reported the following income statement data (presented in partial form):

| | |
|---|---:|
| Operating income | $250,000 |
| Interest expense | ( 50,000) |
| Earnings before tax | 200,000 |
| Income tax | ( 80,000) |
| Net income | $120,000 |

On July 1, 2002, the common stock was split 3 for 1. During 2002, all appropriate dividends were declared and paid on preferred stock and common stock. The common stock dividends were as follows:

| | |
|---|---|
| 1st Quarter | $.21 |
| 2nd Quarter | $.21 |
| 3rd Quarter | $.08 |
| 4th Quarter | $.08 |

The year-end market price was $20.00.

**Required:** For 2002, compute:
- a. basic earnings per share
- b. dividends per share based on ending shares
- c. the degree of financial leverage
- d. percentage of earnings retained
- e. dividend payout
- f. dividend yield
- g. price/earnings ratio
- h. book value per share

Chapter 9 - Problem 7 - Stock Splits and Earnings Per Share

Mike Szabo Corporation reported basic earnings per share of $4.50 in 2001.  In 2002, Mike Szabo Corporation reported basic earnings per share of $2.00.  A three-for-one stock split was declared on October 1, 2002.

**Required:**   a.  Present the basic earnings per share for a two-year comparative income statement that includes 2001 and 2002.

                  b.  Comment on the trend for basic earnings per share.

Chapter 9 - Problem 8 - Earnings Per Share

The following data relate to Hawk Company for the current year:

      18,000 shares of common stock outstanding at the beginning of the year

      April 1 - issued 4,500 shares of common stock

      July 1 - declared 2-for-1 stock split

      $2,000 in preferred dividends paid during the past year

      $60,000 net income

      Average market price on common stock during the past year, $16

      Year-end market price on common stock, $18

**Required:**  Compute the basic earnings per share.

# Chapter 9 - Problem 9 - Earnings Per Share

The following data relate to the Ruth Company for the current
year:

| | |
|---|---:|
| Income before extraordinary item and accounting change | $5,000,000 |
| | |
| Less: Preferred stock dividends | (50,000) |
| Income available to common stockholders | $4,950,000 |
| Extraordinary item | (1,000,000) |
| Accounting change | 2,000,000 |
| Net income available to common stockholders | $5,950,000 |
| | |
| Common shares outstanding on January 1 | 2,000,000 |
| Issuance of common stock on July 1 | 200,000 |

Note: The Ruth Company uses the calendar year.

**Required:**  a.  Compute the weighted-average share.

b.  Compute the basic EPS for:
1.  Income before extraordinary item and
    accounting change.
2.  Extraordinary item.
3.  Accounting change.
4.  Net income.

**CHAPTER 9 - SOLUTIONS**

Chapter 9 - Problem 1 - Supply the Words Necessary to Complete
the Following Items

1. earned; paid

2. net income

3. trading on the equity; higher

4. low; high

5. high; for; against

6. common stock

7. common stockholders

8. not; funds; number

9. P/E; common stock; share

10. diluted; nonrecurring

11. low; losses

12. internal growth

13. share; dividends

14. dividends; market price

15. limited; historical

16. cash; stock; future

17. noncompensatory; compensatory

18. dividends; appreciation

Chapter 9 - Problem 2 - Multiple Choice

__c__   1.                                                    2003      2002     2001
        EPS previously reported                                         $1.00     .80

        2000 declared a 4-for-1
           stock split                                                    .25     .20

        2000 reported .30 EPS                               .30          .25     .20

__d__   2. Price earnings ratio = Market Price Per Share
                                   Fully Diluted Earnings
                                   Per Share

                                   $40 = 20
                                    2

        Dividend payout =   Dividends Per Common Share
                            Fully Diluted Earnings Per Share

                            $1 = 50%
                            $2

__e__   3. Total Stockholders' Equity - Preferred Stock Equity
                  Number of Common Shares Outstanding

        Common stock                        $200,000
        Retained earnings                    250,000
                                            $450,000

        Number of common shares              5,000

                                            $90

__e__   4.                                  Year 1     Year 2     Year 3
           Market price                      $20        $30        $25
           Option price                       20         20         20
                                            -0-         10          5
           Shares                           10,000     10,000     10,000
           Total compensation expense       -0-       100,000     50,000
           Less prior years'
             recognized compensation
             expense                                    -0-      (100,000)
           Compensation expense             -0-       100,000    (50,000)

__d__   5. New EBIT                         $2,000,000
           Prior EBIT                        1,000,000
                                            $1,000,000
           financial leverage                    1.5
                                            $1,500,000

_d_ 6. Adjust the shares in 2002 by adding 10% additional shares. Divide the previous number of shares for 2002 by the new number of shares. This is the percentage of the previous reported earnings per share that should be reported as the adjusted earnings per share.

For illustration, assume the following:

| | | |
|---|---|---|
| (A) | previous 2002 shares | 100,000 |
| | 10% stock dividend | 10,000 |
| (B) | new number of shares | 110,000 |

$$\frac{(A)}{(B)} \quad \frac{100,000}{110,000} = .909$$

_c_ 7. The price/earnings ratio usually reflects investors opinions of the future prospects for the firm.

_d_ 8. Degree of financial leverage gives a perspective on risk in the capital structure.

_e_ 9. Earnings Before Interest, Tax, Minority Share of Earnings, Equity Income, and Nonrecurring Items
——————————————————————————————
Earnings Before Tax, Minority Share of Earnings, Equity Income, and Nonrecurring Items

| | | |
|---|---|---|
| Earnings before tax | | $195,000 |
| Interest | | 8,000 |
| | (A) | $203,000 |
| Earnings before tax | (B) | $195,000 |

$$(A) \div (B) \quad 1.04$$

_c_ 10. The earnings per share ratio is computed for common stock.

_c_ 11. The immediate effect of granting stock options is that it creates the potential that those receiving the options may purchase the stock at a favorable price.

_a_ 12. $P/E = \dfrac{\text{Market Price Per Share}}{\text{Diluted Earnings Per Share}}$

$$\frac{\$30}{\$1.80} = 16.67$$

$$\text{Dividend payout} = \frac{\text{Dividends Per Common Share}}{\text{Diluted Earnings Per Share}}$$

$$\frac{\$1.20}{\$1.80} = 66.67\%$$

___c___ 13. $\dfrac{\text{Total Stockholders' Equity - Preferred Stock Equity}}{\text{Number of Common Shares Outstanding}}$

$$\frac{\$200,000}{\$5,000} = \$40$$

___b___ 14. Increasing financial leverage can be a risky strategy from the viewpoint of stockholders of companies having low and falling profits.

___a___ 15. 10% x 1.3 = 13%

___b___ 16. Dividend yield represents dividends per common share in relation to market price per common share.

___e___ 17. Book value per share may not approximate market value per share because of all of the reasons listed.

___c___ 18. $\dfrac{\text{Net Income - All Dividends}}{\text{Net Income}}$

$$\frac{\$40,000 - \$20,000 - \$5,000}{\$40,000} = 37.50\%$$

___a___ 19. $\dfrac{\text{Dividends Per Common Share}}{\text{Market Price Per Common Share}}$

$$\frac{.70}{\$15.00} = 4.67\%$$

Chapter 9 - Problem 3 - True/False

| | | | | | | | |
|---|---|---|---|---|---|---|---|
| F | 1. | F | 8. | T | 15. | F | 22. |
| T | 2. | T | 9. | F | 16. | T | 23. |
| F | 3. | T | 10. | F | 17. | F | 24. |
| F | 4. | F | 11. | T | 18. | F | 25. |
| T | 5. | T | 12. | F | 19. | | |
| F | 6. | F | 13. | T | 20. | | |
| T | 7. | T | 14. | T | 21. | | |

## Chapter 9 - Problem 4 - Matching Computation of Ratios

| | | | |
|---|---|---|---|
| g | 1. | c | 5. |
| e | 2. | d | 6. |
| a | 3. | f | 7. |
| b | 4. | | |

## Chapter 9 - Problem 5 - Effect of a Transaction on a Given Ratio

| | | | |
|---|---|---|---|
| – | 1. | – | 5. |
| + | 2. | + | 6. |
| – | 3. | | |
| + | 4. | | |

## Chapter 9 - Problem 6 - Computation of Ratios

a.  Earnings per share = $\dfrac{\text{Net Income} - \text{Preferred Dividends}}{\text{Common Shares Outstanding}}$

$$\frac{\$120,000 - \$4,200}{120,000 \,(\text{after split})} = \frac{\$115,800}{120,000} = \$.965$$

b.  Dividends per share:

| | | |
|---|---|---|
| 1st Quarter | $.07 | adjusted for split |
| 2nd Quarter | $.07 | adjusted for split |
| 3rd Quarter | .08 | |
| 4th Quarter | .08 | |

c.  Degree of financial leverage = $\dfrac{\text{EBIT}}{\text{EBT}}$

$$\frac{\$250,000}{\$200,000} = 1.25$$

d.  Percentage of earnings retained = $\dfrac{\text{Net Income} - \text{Dividends}}{\text{Net Income}}$

| | | |
|---|---|---|
| Dividends: | | |
| Preferred stock | | $ 4,200 |
| Common stock | | |
| 1st Quarter .07¢ x 120,000 | 8,400 | |
| 2nd Quarter .07¢ x 120,000 | 8,400 | |
| 3rd Quarter .08¢ x 120,000 | 9,600 | |
| 4th Quarter .08¢ x 120,000 | 9,600 | 36,000 |
| | | $40,200 |

$$\frac{\$120,000 - \$40,200}{\$120,000} = \frac{\$79,800}{\$120,000} = 66.50\%$$

e. Dividend payout $= \dfrac{\text{Dividends Per Common Share}}{\text{Earnings Per Share}} = \dfrac{\$.30}{\$.965} = 31.09\%$

f. Dividend yield $= \dfrac{\text{Dividends Per Common Share}}{\text{Market Price Per Share}} = \dfrac{\$.30}{\$20.00} = 1.50\%$

g. Price/earnings ratio $= \dfrac{\text{Market Price Per Common Share}}{\text{Earnings Per Share}}$

$$\frac{\$20.00}{\$.965} = 20.73 \text{ times}$$

h. Book value per share $= \dfrac{\text{Common Equity}}{\text{Common Shares Outstanding}}$

| | |
|---|---:|
| Beginning retained earnings | $220,000 |
| + Net income | 120,000 |
| | 340,000 |
| – Dividends | 40,200 |
| | 299,800 |
| Plus: | |
| Common stock | 400,000 |
| Paid-in capital | 200,000 |
| Total common equity | $899,800 (A) |
| Common shares | 120,000 (B) |

Book value (A)/(B): $\dfrac{\$899,800}{120,000} = \$7.50$

Chapter 9 - Problem 7 - Stock Splits and Earnings Per Share

a.    Revision of 2001 earnings per share:

          2001 reported earnings per share          $4.50

          October 1, 2002 stock split          x   1/3
          Adjusted 2001 earnings per share          $1.50

                    Comparative Earnings Per Share

                              2002              2001
          Earnings per share  $2.00             $1.50

b.    There was a substantial increase in earnings per share.


Chapter 9 - Problem 8 - Earnings Per Share

a.    Weighted average shares outstanding:
          January 1 18,000 x 1/4          =          4,500
          April 1 Issue 4,500 shares
             New balance
                22,500 x 9/12             =          16,875
                                                     21,375
          July 1 - 2-for-1 stock split                    2
          Weighted average shares                    42,750  (B)

      Income allocated to common stock:

          Net income                                 $60,000
          Less:
             Preferred dividends                       2,000
          Income allocated to common stock           $58,000  (A)

      Basic earnings per share
         (A) divided by (B)                           $1.36


                              216

Chapter 9 - Problem 9 - Earnings Per Share

a.

| Dates<br>Outstanding | Shares<br>Outstanding | Fraction<br>of Period | Weighted-<br>Average Share |
|---|---|---|---|
| January 1 - June 30 | 2,000,000 | ½ | 1,000,000 |
| July 1 - December 31 | 2,200,000 | ½ | 1,100,000 |
| Weighted - average shares | | | 2,100,000 |

b.    Basic EPS for:
      1.    Income before extraordinary
            item and accounting change          $2.36

$$\frac{\$4,950,000}{2,100,000} = \$2.357$$

      2.    Extraordinary item

$$\frac{(\$1,000,000)}{2,100,000} = 4.76 \qquad (.48)$$

      3.    Accounting change

$$\frac{\$2,000,000}{2,100,000} = .952 \qquad .95$$

      4.    Net income

$$\frac{\$5,950,000}{2,100,000} = 2.833 \qquad \$2.83$$

217

# Chapter 10: Statement of Cash Flows

## Chapter 10 - Problem 1 - Supply the Words Necessary to Complete the Following Items

1.  The statement of cash flows is a relatively new statement that did not become required until _____.

2.  FASB Statement No. 95, "Statement of Cash Flows," directs that (1) the statement be prepared on a _____ basis; (2) the title be changed to "The Statement of Cash Flows"; and (3) a fairly _____ and _____ format be used.

3.  All transactions having _____ _____ effects must be reported on the statement of cash flows.

4.  The statement of cash flows classifies cash receipts and cash payments by _____, _____, and _____ _____.

5.  Operating activities include all transactions and other events that are not _____ and _____ activities.

6.  _____ _____ include lending money and collecting on those loans and acquiring and selling investments and productive long-term assets.

7.  _____ _____ include cash flows relating to liability and owners' equity.

8.  Three techniques may be used to complete the steps in developing the statement of cash flows: (1) the _____ _____, (2) the __-_____ method, (3) and the _____ method.

9.  There are two methods of presenting cash flow from operating activities: the _____ and _____ methods.

10. When the cash provided by operations is presented using the direct approach, the income statement accounts are usually described in terms of _____ and _____.

11. To compute cash flows from operations using the indirect approach, we start with _____ _____ and add back or deduct adjustments necessary to change the income on the accrual basis to income on a cash basis, after eliminating gains or losses that relate to _____ or _____ activities.

12. The operating cash flow/current maturities of long-term debt and current notes payable ratio is a ratio that indicates a firm's ability to meet its _____ _____ of debt.

13. The operating cash flow/total debt ratio indicates a firm's ability to cover total _____ with the yearly _____ flow.

14. Operating cash flow per share indicates the funds flow per _____ _____ outstanding.

15. Operating cash flow per share is usually substantially _____ than earnings per share because depreciation has not been _____.

16. The operating cash flow/cash dividends ratio indicates a firm's ability to cover _____ _____ with the yearly operating _____ _____.

17. There is ___ standard definition of cash flow.


Chapter 10 - Problem 2 - Multiple Choice

Choose the best answer for each of the following questions and enter the identifying letter in the space provided.

_____ 1. Why is depreciation added to income in the operations section of the statement of cash flows? (Cash flow from operations computed using the indirect approach.)

   a. Depreciation is not an expense.
   b. Depreciation does not require an outlay of funds.
   c. Depreciation is not tax deductible.
   d. Depreciation increases income.
   e. Depreciation is an expense item.

_____ 2. Which of the following is **not** a typical cash flow under operating activities?

    a. Cash inflows from sale of goods or services
    b. Cash inflows from interest
    c. Cash outflows to employees
    d. Cash outflows to suppliers
    e. Cash inflows from sale of property, plant, and equipment

_____ 3. A transaction that will increase working capital is:

    a. purchase of marketable securities
    b. payment of accounts payable
    c. collection of accounts receivable
    d. sale of common stock
    e. none of the above

_____ 4. Which of the following is a primary purpose of the statement of cash flows?

    a. To show cash flow from operations, financing activities, and investing activities.
    b. To show the change in working capital.
    c. To show revenue and expense for a selected time period.
    d. To show stock dividends.
    e. None of the above.

_____ 5. Which of the following is a typical cash flow under operating activities?

    a. cash outflow for purchase of property, plant, and equipment
    b. cash outflows to suppliers
    c. cash inflow from selling long-term investments
    d. cash outflow for dividends paid
    e. none of the above

_____ 6. Which of the following is a typical cash flow under investing activities?

    a. payment on bonds payable
    b. payment for purchase of bonds
    c. retirement of preferred stock
    d. payment to supplier
    e. none of the above

_____ 7. Working capital is defined as:

    a. current assets less current liabilities.
    b. cash equivalent accounts less current liabilities.
    c. current assets less notes payable.
    d. total assets less current liabilities.
    e. current assets less cash equivalent accounts.

_____ 8. Amortization of goodwill can be added back to income in the operations section of the statement of cash flows:

    a. because it represents a cash inflow.
    b. because amortization of goodwill does not require an outlay of funds.
    c. goodwill amortization is not an expense.
    d. goodwill amortization represents a cash outflow.
    e. none of the above.

_____ 9. Which of the following is **not** an item added back to income in the operations section of the statement of cash flows when using the indirect presentation?

    a. amortization of patents
    b. increase in inventory
    c. decrease in accounts receivable
    d. increase in accounts payable
    e. depreciation

_____ 10. Management should use the statement of cash flows for which of the following purposes?

    a. Determine the financial position.
    b. Determine cash flow from investing activities.
    c. Determine the balance in accounts payable.
    d. Determine the balance in accounts receivable.
    e. None of the above.

_____ 11. Jones Company had sales of $250,000, decrease in accounts payable of $10,000, decrease in accounts receivable of $5,000, decrease in inventories of $5,000, and patent amortization of $5,000. What was the cash collected from customers?

    a. $255,000
    b. $245,000
    c. $250,000
    d. $260,000
    e. $240,000

_____ 12. Smith Company had net income of $20,000, increase in accounts payable of $4,000, increase in accounts receivable of $2,000, decrease in inventories of $3,000, and depreciation expense of $5,000. What was the cash from operations?

a. $28,000
b. $18,000
c. $34,000
d. $22,000
e. none of the above

_____ 13. Schrader Company had sales of $40,000, decrease in accounts payable of $3,000, decrease in accounts receivable of $4,000, tax expense of $8,000, increase in deferred tax liability of $3,000, and an increase in taxes payable of $2,000. What was the cash outflow for taxes?

a. $3,000
b. $9,000
c. $7,000
d. $13,000
e. none of the above

_____ 14. The purchase of land by the issuance of bonds payable should be presented in a statement of cash flows in which of the following sections?

a. cash flows from operating activities
b. supplemental schedule of noncash investing and financing activities
c. cash flows from investing activities
d. cash flows from financing activities
e. none of the above

_____ 15. Which of the following accounts is **not** part of working capital?

a. cash
b. prepaid insurance
c. accounts payable
d. wages payable
e. equipment

Questions 16-19 are based on the following information:

Fox Company
Balance Sheet (Partial)
December 31, 2002 and 2001

| (Dollars in thousands) | 2002 | 2001 |
|---|---|---|
| Assets: | | |
| Current assets | | |
| Total current assets | $143,809 | $191,472 |
| Other assets | 9,068 | 7,725 |
| Property, plant & equipment, net | 74,574 | 90,087 |
| Intangible assets | 98,771 | 104,266 |
| Total assets | $326,222 | $393,550 |
| | | |
| Liabilities and Shareholders' Equity: | | |
| Current liabilities: | | |
| Short-term borrowings | $ 16,753 | $ 52,719 |
| Trade accounts payable | 26,242 | 34,225 |
| Payrolls and other compensation | 11,922 | 12,486 |
| Other accrued liabilities | 19,355 | 17,627 |
| Income taxes | 7,233 | 8,720 |
| Current maturities on long-term debt | 4,233 | 723 |
| Total current liabilities | 85,738 | 126,500 |
| | | |
| Long-term debt | 114,387 | 141,755 |
| | | |
| Deferred liabilities | 9,293 | 9,845 |
| | | |
| Shareholders' equity: | | |
| Capital stock, 10,500,000 | | |
| shares issued and outstanding | 23,348 | 24,170 |
| Retained earnings | 93,456 | 91,280 |
| Total shareholders' equity | 116,804 | 115,450 |
| Total liabilities and shareholders' equity | $326,222 | $393,550 |

223

## Fox Company
## Income Statement (Partial)
### Years Ended December 31, 2002, 2001, and 2000

| (Dollars in thousands, except per share amounts) | 2002 | 2001 | 2000 |
|---|---|---|---|
| Net sales | $433,968 | $445,398 | $246,221 |
| Cost of products sold | (267,265) | (263,338) | (145,241) |
| Gross profit | 166,703 | 182,060 | 100,980 |
| Operating expenses | (124,061) | (121,952) | ( 67,959) |
| Earnings before other expenses and income taxes | 42,642 | 60,108 | 33,021 |
| Other expense | (25,695) | (25,743) | ( 68) |
| Earnings before income taxes | 16,947 | 34,365 | 32,953 |
| Income taxes | ( 9,105 | (14,802 | ( 13,125) |
| Net earnings | $ 7,842 | $ 19,563 | $ 19,828 |
| Basic net income per common share | $.60 | $1.48 | $1.51 |

## Fox Company
## Statements of Cash Flows (Partial)
### Years Ended December 31, 2002, 2001, and 2000

| (Dollars in thousands) | 2002 | 2001 | 2000 |
|---|---|---|---|
| Net cash provided by operating activities | $ 33,064 | $ 10,678 | $ 1,897 |
| Net cash provided by (used in) investing activities | 972 | (24,187) | (96,985) |
| Net cash provided by (used in) financing activities* | (36,790) | ( 715) | 113,018 |
| Effect of exchange rate changes on cash | ( 162) | 859 | ( 310) |
| Net increase (decrease) in cash and cash equivalents | ( 2,916) | (13,365) | 17,620 |
| Cash and cash equivalents: | | | |
| Beginning of year | 6,520 | 19,885 | 2,265 |
| End of year | $ 3,604 | $ 6,520 | $ 19,885 |

*Includes dividends of $2,040, $1,596, and $1,639 respectively.

_____ 16. What is the Operating Cash Flow/Current Maturities of Long-Term Debt and Current Notes Payable ratio for 2002?

      a.  57.55%
      b.  197.36%
      c.  157.55%
      d.  219.60%
      e.  none of the above

_____ 17. What is the Operating Cash Flow/Total Debt ratio for 2002?

      a.  15.79%
      b.  17.57%
      c.  38.56%
      d.  16.52%
      e.  none of the above

_____ 18. What is the Operating Cash Flow Per Share ratio for 2002?

      a.  $3.15
      b.  $3.68
      c.  $3.20
      d.  $3.25
      e.  none of the above

_____ 19. What is the Operating Cash Flow/Cash Dividends for 2002?

      a.  20.00
      b.   6.21
      c.  18.03
      d.  16.21
      e.  none of the above

## Chapter 10 - Problem 3 - True/False

Indicate whether each of the following is true (T) or false (F) in the space provided.

_____ 1. The statement of cash flows classifies cash receipts and cash payments by operating, investing, and financing activities.

_____ 2. Cash flows from operating activities are generally the cash effects of transactions and other events that enter into the determination of net income.

_____ 3. A build-up of receivables would increase net working capital, but this would not increase cash or the cash equivalents.

_____ 4. The all-financial resources approach should be used in the preparation of the statement of cash flows.

_____ 5. In your primary analysis, consider funds provided by operations excluding the nonrecurring items.

_____ 6. Depreciation is deducted from income in the process of computing cash from operations.

_____ 7. A one-year period can be misleading as to how a company obtains cash and how it uses cash.

_____ 8. Because many of the items on the statement of cash flows do not appear each year, it is difficult to do a meaningful horizontal common-size statement for the entire statement.

_____ 9. There is a standard definition of cash flow.

_____ 10. In the short-run, cash flow per share is a better indication of a firm's ability to pay dividends than is earnings per share.

_____ 11. The requirement of issuing a statement that presented a flow of cash is rather recent.

_____ 12. Working capital is not considered to be an indicator of liquidity.

_____ 13. The income statement will fairly represent the cash flow from operations.

_____ 14. When the direct method of presenting cash flow from operations is used, the income statement is essentially presented on a cash receipts and cash payments basis.

_____ 15. The cash flow/current maturities of long-term debt and current notes payable ratio is a ratio that indicates short-term debt-paying ability.

_____ 16. Cash flow per share is usually lower than earnings per share.

_____ 17. Cash flow per share can be viewed as a substitute for earnings per share.

_____ 18. SFAS No. 95 uses a broad concept of cash.

_____ 19. A supporting schedule to the statement of cash flows may include noncash flow items.

_____ 20.  Sale of equipment for cash is an operating activity.

_____ 21.  The acquisition of land using notes payable is an example of a noncash transaction.

_____ 22.  Payment of cash dividends is an operating activity.

_____ 23.  The purchase of equipment using cash is an investing activity.

Chapter 10 - Problem 4 - Matching Computation of Ratios

Listed below are several ratios.  Match the letter that goes with each formula.

a.  operating cash flow/current maturities of long-term debt and current notes payable
b.  operating cash flow/total debt
c.  operating cash flow per share
d.  operating cash flow/cash dividends

_____ 1.  $$\frac{\text{Operating Cash Flow}}{\text{Cash Dividends}}$$

_____ 2.  $$\frac{\text{Operating Cash Flow}}{\text{Total Debt}}$$

_____ 3.  $$\frac{\text{Operating Cash Flow}}{\text{Current Maturities of Long - Term Debt and Current Notes Payable}}$$

_____ 4.  $$\frac{\text{Operating Cash Flow - Preferred Dividends}}{\text{Common Shares Outstanding}}$$

## Chapter 10 - Problem 5 - Effect of Selected Transactions on Cash and Working Capital

Indicate the effect of each of the following transactions on (a) cash and (b) working capital.  Use a + to indicate an increase, - to indicate a decrease, and 0 for no effect.

|  |  | Cash | Working Capital |
|---|---|---|---|
| 1. | payment of accounts payable |  |  |
| 2. | purchase of land for cash |  |  |
| 3. | sell preferred stock for cash |  |  |
| 4. | decrease in deferred taxes (long-term liability) |  |  |
| 5. | amortization of discount on bonds payable |  |  |
| 6. | amortization of patents |  |  |
| 7. | pay long-term bonds payable |  |  |
| 8. | collection of accounts receivable |  |  |

## Chapter 10 - Problem 6 - Identify Presentation

Indicate whether each of the following would be under Operating (O), Investing (I), Financing (F), or whether the item would not appear (N) on the Statement of Cash Flows.

_____ a.  net income
_____ b.  purchase of fixed assets
_____ c.  increase in accounts payable
_____ d.  issuance of long-term debt
_____ e.  depreciation
_____ f.  dividends paid
_____ g.  sale of fixed assets
_____ h.  decrease in accounts receivable
_____ i.  increase in short-term borrowings

# Chapter 10 - Problem 7 - Converting Accrual Basis Income Statement To Cash Basis Income Statement

Using the accrual basis income statement and the additional data prepare a cash basis income statement.

Rocket Company
Accrual Basis Income Statement
For the Year Ended December 31, 2000

| | |
|---|---:|
| Sales | $300,000 |
| Operating expenses | 160,000 |
| Operating income | 140,000 |
| Loss on sale of building | (20,000) |
| Income before tax expense | 120,000 |
| Tax expense | 45,000 |
| Net income | $ 75,000 |
| Additional data: | |
| Depreciation expense | $ 4,500 |
| Decrease in accounts receivable | 5,000 |
| Decrease in inventories | 6,000 |
| Increase in prepaid expenses | 2,000 |
| Increase in long-term other assets (not related to cash flow from operations | 1,000 |
| Increase in accounts payable | 2,000 |
| Increase in accrued liabilities | 3,000 |
| Increase in income taxes payable | 4,000 |
| Increase in preferred stock | 10,000 |

# Chapter 10 - Problem 8 - Prepare the Statement of Cash Flows and Selected Ratios

The balance sheet for December 31, 2002, and December 31, 2001, and the income statement for the year ended December 31, 2002, of Growth Company follow:

| Assets: | 2002 | 2001 |
|---|---|---|
| Cash | $ 40,000 | $ 30,000 |
| Accounts receivable, net | 70,000 | 75,000 |
| Inventory | 90,000 | 95,000 |
| Land | 80,000 | 80,000 |
| Building and equipment | 120,000 | 100,000 |
| Accumulated depreciation | (80,000) | (70,000) |
| Total assets | $320,000 | $310,000 |

| Liabilities and Stockholders' Equity: | | |
|---|---|---|
| Accounts payable | $ 35,000 | $ 40,000 |
| Income taxes payable | 6,000 | 4,000 |
| Wages payable | 7,000 | 6,000 |
| Current notes payable | 40,000 | 60,000 |
| Common stock | 120,000 | 110,000 |
| Retained earnings | 112,000 | 90,000 |
| Total liabilities and stockholders' Equity | $320,000 | $310,000 |

Growth Company
Income Statement
For the Year Ended December 31, 2002

| | |
|---|---|
| Sales | $650,000 |
| Less expenses: | |
| Cost of goods sold | (460,000) |
| Selling and administrative expenses (includes depreciation of $10,000) | (120,000) |
| Interest expense | ( 6,000) |
| Income before income taxes | 64,000 |
| Income tax expense | ( 25,000) |
| Net income | $ 39,000 |

Note: Cash dividends of $17,000 were paid during 2002.

**Required:** a. Prepare the statement of cash flows for 2002. (Present cash flows from operations using the indirect approach.)

b. Compute the ratio cash flow/current maturities of long-term debt and current notes payable.

# CHAPTER 10 - SOLUTIONS

## Chapter 10 - Problem 1 - Supply the Words Necessary to Complete the Following Items

1.  1988

2.  cash; specific; detailed

3.  cash flow

4.  operating, investing; financing activities

5.  investing; financing

6.  Investing activities

7.  Financing activities

8.  visual method; T-account; worksheet

9.  direct; indirect

10. receipts; payments

11. net income; investing; financing

12. current maturities

13. debt; cash

14. common share

15. higher; deducted

16. cash dividends; cash flow

17. no


## Chapter 10 - Problem 2 - Multiple Choice

__b__   1.  Depreciation has been deducted when computing income. Depreciation does not represent a cash outflow.

__e__   2.  Cash inflows from sale of property, plant, and equipment represents cash inflows related to investing activities.

__d__   3.  The sale of common stock will increase working capital.

| a | 4. | A primary purpose of the statement of cash flows is to show cash flow from operations, financing activities, and investing activities. |
|---|---|---|
| b | 5. | Cash outflows to suppliers is a typical cash flow under operating actvities. |
| b | 6. | Payment for purchase of bonds is a typical cash flow under investing activities. |
| a | 7. | Working capital is defined as current assets less current liabilities. |
| b | 8. | Amortization of goodwill can be added back to income in the operations section of the statement of cash flows because amortization of goodwill does not require an outlay of funds. |
| b | 9. | Increase in inventory is subtracted from income in the operations section of the statement of cash flows when using the indirect presentation. |
| b | 10. | Management should use the statement of cash flows to determine cash flow from investing activities. |

| a | 11. | Sales | $250,000 |
|---|---|---|---|
|  |  | Add decrease in accounts receivable | 5,000 |
|  |  |  | $255,000 |

| e | 12. | Net income | $ 20,000 |
|---|---|---|---|
|  |  | Add increase in accounts payable | 4,000 |
|  |  | Deduct increase in accounts receivable | ( 2,000) |
|  |  | Add decrease in inventories | 3,000 |
|  |  | Add depreciation expense | 5,000 |
|  |  |  | $ 30,000 |

| a | 13. | Tax expense | $ 8,000 |
|---|---|---|---|
|  |  | Increase in deferred tax liabilities | ( 3,000) |
|  |  | Increase in taxes payable | ( 2,000) |
|  |  | Cash outflow for taxes | $ 3,000 |

| b | 14. | This is a noncash investing and financing activity. |
|---|---|---|
| e | 15. | Equipment is not part of working capital. |

| c | 16. | Net cash provided by operating activities | | $ 33,064 |
|---|---|---|---|---|
| | | Short-term borrowings | $ 16,753 | |
| | | Current maturities on long-term debt | 4,233 | 20,986 |

$$= 157.55\%$$

| a | 17. | Net cash provided by operating activities | | $ 33,064 |
|---|---|---|---|---|
| | | Total current liabilities | $ 85,738 | |
| | | Long-term debt | 114,387 | |
| | | Deferred liabilities | 9,293 | 209,418 |

$$= 15.79\%$$

| a | 18. | Net cash provided by operating activities | $33,064,000 | = $3.15 |
|---|---|---|---|---|
| | | Shares issued and outstanding | 10,500,000 | |

| d | 19. | Net cash provided by operating activities | $33,064 | = 16.21 times |
|---|---|---|---|---|
| | | Cash dividends | $ 2,040 | |

## Chapter 10 - Problem 3 - True/False

| | | | | | | | | |
|---|---|---|---|---|---|---|---|---|
| T | 1. | | | | F | 16. | | |
| T | 2. | F | 9. | | F | 17. | | |
| T | 3. | T | 10. | | T | 18. | | |
| T | 4. | T | 11. | | T | 19. | | |
| T | 5. | F | 12. | | F | 20. | | |
| F | 6. | F | 13. | | T | 21. | | |
| T | 7. | T | 14. | | F | 22. | | |
| T | 8. | T | 15. | | T | 23. | | |

## Chapter 10 - Problem 4 - Matching Computation of Ratios

| d | 1. |
|---|---|
| b | 2. |
| a | 3. |
| c | 4. |

## Chapter 10 - Problem 5 - Effect of Selected Transactions on Cash and Working Capital

|     |                                                    | Cash | Working Capital |
| --- | -------------------------------------------------- | :--: | :-------------: |
| 1.  | payment of accounts payable                        |  −   |        0        |
| 2.  | purchase of land for cash                          |  −   |        −        |
| 3.  | sell preferred stock for cash                      |  +   |        +        |
| 4.  | decrease in deferred taxes (long-term liability)   |  0   |        0        |
| 5.  | amortization of discount on bonds payable          |  0   |        0        |
| 6.  | amortization of patents                            |  0   |        0        |
| 7.  | pay long-term bonds payable                        |  −   |        −        |
| 8.  | collection of accounts receivable                  |  +   |        0        |

## Chapter 10 - Problem 6 - Identify Presentation

| | |
| :--: | --- |
| O | a. |
| I | b. |
| O | c. |
| F | d. |
| O | e. |
| F | f. |
| I | g. |
| O | h. |
| F | i. |

Chapter 10 - Problem 7 - Converting Accrual Basis Income Statement To Cash Basis Income Statement

|  | Accrual Basis | Adjustments | Add (Subtract) | Cash Basis |
|---|---|---|---|---|
| Sales | $300,000 | Decrease in accounts receivable | 5,000 | $305,000 |
| Operating expenses | 160,000 | Depreciation expense | (4,500) |  |
|  |  | Decrease in inventories | (6,000) |  |
|  |  | Increase in prepaid expenses | 2,000 |  |
|  |  | Increase in accounts payable | (2,000) |  |
|  |  | Increase in accrued liabilities | (3,000) | 146,500 |
| Operating income | 140,000 |  |  | 158,500 |
| Loss on sale of building | (20,000) | This loss is related to investing activities | 20,000 | - 0 - |
| Income before tax expense | 120,000 |  |  |  |
| Tax expense | 45,000 | Increase in income taxes payable | (4,000) | 41,000 |
| Net income | $75,000 |  |  | $117,500 |

Rocket Company
Cash Basis Income Statement
For the Year Ended December 31, 2000

| Sales | $305,000 |
|---|---|
| Operating expenses | 146,500 |
| Operating income | 158,500 |
| Tax expense | 41,000 |
| Net income | $117,500 |

Chapter 10 - Problem 8 - Prepare the Statement of Cash Flows
and Selected Ratios

a.                          Growth Company
                      Statement of Cash Flows
                For the Year Ended December 31, 2002

Cash flow from operating activities:
Net income                                                    $ 39,000
Add/(deduct) items not affecting operating cash:
  Depreciation expense                                          10,000
  Decrease in receivables                                        5,000
  Decrease in inventory                                          5,000
  Accounts payable decrease                                     (5,000)
  Income taxes payable increase                                  2,000
  Wages payable increase                                         1,000
Net increase in cash flow from operations                     $ 57,000

Cash flow from investing activities:
  Cash payments for building                                  (20,000)

Cash flow from financing activities:
  Cash from issuance of stock                                   10,000
  Cash paid for retirement of notes payable                   (20,000)
  Cash dividends paid                                          (17,000)
Net cash outflow from financing activities                    (27,000)

Net increase in cash                                          $ 10,000


b.    $\dfrac{\$57,000}{40,000} = 1.43$

# Chapter 11:   Expanded Analysis

Chapter 11 - Problem 1 - Supply the Words Necessary to Complete
                the Following Items

1.  For commercial loan officers, most of the ratios given a
    high significance rating had a primary measure of
    _____ or _____.

2.  The financial executives gave the _____ ratios the
    highest significance ratings.

3.  The CPAs gave the highest significance rating to two
    _____ ratios.

4.  The financial analysts gave the highest significance ratings
    to _____ ratios.

5.  In the annual reports, _____ ratios and ratios
    related to _____ were the most popular.

6.  Accounting policies that result in the slowest reporting of
    income are the most _____.

7.  A univariate model involves the use of a _____ variable
    in a prediction model.

8.  With the Altman model, the _____ the Z score the more
    likely that the firm will go _____.

9.  The objective of analytical review procedures is to isolate
    _____ fluctuations and _____ items in operating
    statistics.

10. For many of the ratios, we _____ generalize about whether
    the ratio will improve or decline when the LIFO reserve is
    used.

11. There are many forms of graphs.  Some popular forms used by
    accountants are _____, _____, _____, and _____.

## Chapter 11 - Problem 2 - Multiple Choice

Choose the best answer for each of the following questions and enter the identifying letter in the space provided.

_____ 1. All but one of these ratios was viewed as a debt ratio by commercial loan officers:

   a. debt/equity
   b. cash flow/current maturities of long-term debt
   c. fixed charge coverage
   d. degree of financial leverage
   e. inventory turnover days

_____ 2. Which of the following ratios is **least** likely to appear in a loan agreement?

   a. debt/equity
   b. current ratio
   c. dividend payout
   d. times interest earned
   e. inventory turnover

_____ 3. Of the five ratios listed below, which one was given the lowest significance rating by controllers?

   a. earnings per share
   b. return on equityCafter tax
   c. debt/equity ratio
   d. dividend payout ratio
   e. quick (acid-test) ratio

_____ 4. The ratio **most** likely to be included in the management discussion section of the annual report is:

   a. debt/equity
   b. current ratio
   c. inventory turnover
   d. dividends per share
   e. times interest earned

_____ 5.  Which of the following would **not** be considered to be a
           conservative accounting policy?

           a.  FIFO inventory, under inflation
           b.  accelerated depreciation
           c.  immediate expensing of research and development
           d.  LIFO inventory, under inflation
           e.  a low rate of interest assumed to be earned on
               pension funds

_____ 6.  A variable that indicates a measure of cumulative
           profitability over time:

           a.  retained earnings (balance sheet)/total assets
           b.  earnings before interest and taxes/total assets
           c.  working capital/total assets
           d.  market value of equity/book value of total debt
           e.  sales/total assets

_____ 7.  In computing the Altman model z score, a working
           capital/total assets of 25% is noted as:

           a.  2.5%
           b.  25%
           c.  250
           d.  25
           e.  2.5

_____ 8.  Which of the following z scores, following the Altman
           model, would a firm **most** likely prefer?

           a.  2.50
           b.  1.90
           c.  1.60
           d.  1.40
           e.   .80

_____ 9.  Which of the following would probably **not** result from
           the use of the LIFO reserve vs. not using the LIFO
           reserve?

|     |                         | Considering LIFO Reserve | Not Considering LIFO Reserve |
| --- | ----------------------- | ------------------------ | ---------------------------- |
| a.  | days' sales in inventory | 60 days                 | 52 days                      |
| b.  | operating cycle          | 110 days                | 90 days                      |
| c.  | current ratio            | 2.1 times               | 1.9 times                    |
| d.  | sales to working capital | 7.4 times               | 6.2 times                    |
| e.  | debt ratio               | 56%                     | 59%                          |

_____ 10. Which of the following statements is **not** true?

    a. A review of the financial statements, including the footnotes, will indicate how conservative the statements are in regard to accounting policies.

    b. Accounting policies that result in the slowest reporting of income are considered to be liberal accounting policies.

    c. When a firm has conservative accounting policies, it is said that its earnings are of high quality.

    d. Under inflationary conditions, the most conservative inventory method is LIFO.

    e. none of the above.

_____ 11. Which of the following is **not** a reasonable matching?

| | Item | Related Conservative Policy |
|---|---|---|
| a. | inventory | LIFO |
| b. | fixed assets | accelerated depreciation |
| c. | intangible assets | short period of time for amortization |
| d. | pensions | short period of time to amortize prior service cost |
| e. | leases (lessee) | material amount of operating leases |

_____ 12. The Beaver Study indicated the following ratio (ratios) to be the best for forecasting financial failure:

    a. cash flow/total debt

    b. net income/total assets

    c. total debt/total assets

    d. a and b only

    e. a, b, and c

Chapter 11 - Problem 3 - True/False

Indicate whether each of the following is true (T) or false (F) in the space provided.

_____ 1. Commercial loan officers gave the debt/equity ratio the highest significance rating.

_____ 2. Commercial loan officers rated the dividend payout ratio to be a highly significant ratio.

_____ 3. Profitability ratios are likely to appear in loan agreements.

_____ 4. The one ratio that appears in the top ten ratios as rated by controllers, but not in the top ten of ratios used for corporate objectives was the ratio price/earnings ratio.

_____ 5. Controllers indicated a better balance in terms of ratios used in corporate objectives than they did in terms of significant ratios.

_____ 6. In general, firms have made good use of the data disclosed in the annual report.

_____ 7. We would always expect earnings per share to be disclosed in the annual report.

_____ 8. Computational methodology is not a problem with financial ratios disclosed in annual reports.

_____ 9. Goodwill results when a firm buys another firm and pays a price that is more than the value of the identifiable assets.

_____ 10. Accounting for extensive assets as operating leases rather than capital leases or with debt results in a permanently more favorable income.

_____ 11. One of the problems in examining the literature that deals with forecasting financial failure is that different authors have used different criteria to indicate failure.

_____ 12. A univariate model of forecasting financial failure involves the use of a single variable in a prediction model.

_____ 13. Failed firms tend to have more inventory one year before failure than nonfailed firms.

_____ 14. The Altman model is not likely to be useful for a firm that has little trading activity in its stock.

_____ 15. No conclusive model has yet been developed to forecast financial failure.

_____ 16. Horizontal and vertical common-size analysis can be effectively used in analytical review procedures.

_____ 17. A proposed comprehensive budget should be compared with financial ratios that have been agreed upon as part of the firm's corporate objectives.

_____ 18. Adding the gross increase in a LIFO reserve to the reported income results in an approximate income if inventory had been valued at approximate current costs.

_____ 19. The sales to working capital ratio would usually increase when the statements are adjusted for the LIFO reserve account.

_____ 20. Most firms use inflation ratios in corporate objectives.

_____ 21. In general, no regulatory agency such as The Securities and Exchange Commission or the Financial Accounting Standards Board accepts responsibility for determining either the content of financial ratios or the format of presentation in annual reports.

_____ 22. The straight-line depreciation method is a conservative depreciation method.

_____ 23. A univariate model to predict financial failure uses multiple variables to predict financial failure.

_____ 24. With the Altman model, the lower the z score the more likely that the firm will go bankrupt.

_____ 25. A column graph is similar to a bar graph.

Chapter 11 - Problem 4 - Ratios Considering LIFO Reserves

Jackie Company presented the following data for 2002 and 2001:

|  | 2002 | 2001 |
|---|---|---|
| Selected balance sheet data: | | |
| Merchandise inventories (LIFO) | $ 36,000 | $ 30,000 |
| Total current assets | $ 74,000 | $ 70,000 |
| Total assets | $120,000 | $110,000 |
| Total current liabilities | $ 36,000 | $ 34,000 |
| Total long-term debt | $ 40,000 | $ 40,000 |
| | | |
| Selected income statement data: | | |
| Net sales | $500,000 | $480,000 |
| Cost of merchandise sold | $305,000 | $284,000 |
| Net income | $ 6,000 | $ 5,000 |
| Net income per common share | $2.90 | $2.70 |
| Effective tax rate | 35% | 35% |

Selected partial footnote with 2002 financial statements:
Inventories have been reduced by $15,000 and $10,000 at December
31, 2002 and December 31, 2001 respectively, from amounts which
would have been reported under the FIFO method (which
approximated current cost).

**Required:** a. Compute the following ratios for 2002 from the
financial statements (using LIFO):
1. Days' sales in inventory
2. Working capital
3. Current ratio
4. Debt ratio

b. Compute the following ratios for 2002 using FIFO
disclosure.
1. Days' sales in inventory
2. Working capital
3. Current ratio
4. Debt ratio

c. Comment on the difference in the indicated
liquidity and debt between the ratios computed
under Lifo and the ratios computed under Fifo.

# Chapter 11 - Problem 5 - Approximate Income If Inventory Had Been Valued At Approximate Current Cost

| | |
|---|---|
| 2001 Net income as reported | $ 80,000,000 |
| 2001 Inventory reserve | $ 38,000,000 |
| 2000 Inventory reserve | $ 32,000,000 |
| 2001 Income taxes | $ 36,000,000 |
| 2001 Income before income taxes | $116,000,000 |

**Required:** Compute the approximate income for 2001 if inventory had been valued at approximate current cost.

## Chapter 11 - Problem 6 - Computation of Z Score

The following data are presented for Data Company:

### Variable

| | |
|---|---|
| Working capital | $ 90,000 |
| Total assets | $620,000 |
| Retained earnings | $ 30,000 |
| Earnings before interest and taxes | $ 55,000 |
| Market value of equity | $100,000 |
| Book value of total debt | $280,000 |
| Sales | $440,000 |

Z score formula:

$$Z = .012X_1 + .014X_2 + .033X_3, + .006X_4 + .010X_5$$

$X_1$ = Working Capital / Total Assets

$X_2$ = Retained Earnings (balance sheet)/Total Assets

$X_3$ = Earnings Before Interest and Taxes/Total Assets

$X_4$ = Market Value of Equity/Book Value of Total Debt

$X_5$ = Sales/Total Assets

**Required:**  a.  Compute the Z score for the Data Company.
b.  Considering the Altman model, comment on the likelihood that this firm will experience financial failures.

Chapter 11 - Problem 7 - Computation of Z Score

Name of firm:   Rocket Company

| | |
|---|---:|
| Current assets | $ 30,000 |
| Total assets | $ 88,000 |
| Current liabilities | $ 18,000 |
| Book value of total debt | $ 38,000 |
| Retained earnings | $ 42,000 |
| Sales | $125,000 |
| Earnings before interest and tax | $ 22,000 |
| Market value of stock | $      30 |
| Number of shares outstanding | 8,000 |

**Required:**  Compute the Z score for Rocket Company.

# CHAPTER 11 - SOLUTIONS

## Chapter 11 - Problem 1 - Supply the Words Necessary to Complete the Following Items

1.  liquidity, debt

2.  profitability

3.  liquidity

4.  profitability

5.  profitability; investing

6.  conservative

7.  single

8.  lower; bankrupt

9.  significant; unusual

10. cannot

11. line, column, bar; pie


## Chapter 11 - Problem 2 - Multiple Choice

___e___  1.  Commercial loan officers viewed inventory turnover days as a liquidity ratio.

___e___  2.  Inventory turnover is least likely to appear in a loan agreement.

___e___  3.  The quick (acid-test) ratio was given the lowest significance rating of the ratios listed here.

___d___  4.  Dividends per share is the ratio most likely to be included in the management discussion section of the annual report.

___a___  5.  FIFO inventory, under inflation would not be considered to be a conservative accounting policy.

___a___  6.  Retained earnings (balance sheet)/total assets indicates a measure of cumulative profitability over time.

| | | | | | | | | | |
|---|---|---|---|---|---|---|---|---|---|
| d | 7. | In computing the Altman model Z score, a working capital/total assets of 25% is noted as 25. |

   d    7.    In computing the Altman model Z score, a working capital/total assets of 25% is noted as 25.

   a    8.    The firm would prefer a high Z score using the Altman model.

   d    9.    Considering LIFO reserve would decrease the sales to working capital because of the increase in inventory.

   b   10.   Accounting policies that result in the slowest reporting of income are considered to be conservative accounting policies.

   e   11.   Accounting for extensive assets as operating leases rather than capital leases or financing with debt, results in a permanently more favorable income.

   e   12.   The Beaver study indicated cash flow/total debt, net income/total assets, and total debt/total assets to be the best for forecasting financial failure.

Chapter 11 - Problem 3 - True/False

| | | | | | | | | | |
|---|---|---|---|---|---|---|---|---|---|
| T | 1. | F | 6. | T | 11. | T | 16. | T | 21. |
| F | 2. | T | 7. | T | 12. | T | 17. | F | 22. |
| F | 3. | F | 8. | F | 13. | F | 18. | F | 23. |
| T | 4. | T | 9. | T | 14. | F | 19. | T | 24. |
| T | 5. | T | 10. | T | 15. | F | 20. | T | 25. |

Chapter 11 - Problem 4 - Ratios Considering LIFO Reserves

a.

1.  Days' Sales In Inventory = $\dfrac{\text{Ending Inventory}}{\text{Cost of Goods Sold} / 365}$

$$\frac{\$36,000}{\$305,000 / 365} = 43.08 \text{ Days}$$

2.  Working Capital = Current Assets - Current Liabilities

$$\$74,000 - \$36,000 = \$38,000$$

3. Current Ratio = $\dfrac{\text{Current Assets}}{\text{Current Liabilities}}$

$$\dfrac{\$74,000}{\$36,000} = 2.06$$

4. Debt Ratio = $\dfrac{\text{Total Liabilities}}{\text{Total Assets}}$

$$\dfrac{\$36,000 + \$40,000}{\$120,000} = \dfrac{\$76,000}{\$120,000} = 63.33\%$$

b.

1. Days' Sales In Inventory = $\dfrac{\text{Ending Inventory}}{\text{Cost of Goods Sold} / 365}$

$$\dfrac{\$36,000 + \$15,000}{(\$305,000 - \$5,000) / 365} = \dfrac{\$51,000}{\$300,000 / 365} = 62.05 \text{ Days}$$

2. Working Capital = Current Assets - Current Liabilities

($74,000 + $15,000) - ($36,000 + $5,250) = $47,750

Increase in tax liabilities
35% x $15,000 = $5,250

3. Current Ratio = $\dfrac{\text{Current Assets}}{\text{Current Liabilities}}$

$$\dfrac{\$74,000 + \$15,000}{\$36,000 + \$5,250} = \dfrac{\$89,000}{\$41,250} = 2.16$$

4. Debt Ratio = $\dfrac{\text{Total Liabilities}}{\text{Total Assets}}$

$$\dfrac{\$36,000 + \$40,000 + \$5,250}{\$120,000 + \$15,000} = \dfrac{\$81,250}{\$135,000} = 60.19\%$$

c. Days' Sales In Inventory
    This ratio indicates that there is substantially more days' sales in inventory than that indicated using LIFO. The adjusted ratio is a better indicator because the

251

inventory figure is closer to current cost than under LIFO.

Working Capital
        The adjusted working capital is substantially higher
than the working capital under LIFO.  The adjusted working
capital is a better indicator because of the more realistic
inventory amount.

Current Ratio
        The adjusted current ratio is higher than the current
ratio computed using the LIFO figures.  The adjusted current
ratio is a better indicator because of the more realistic
inventory.

Debt Ratio
        The adjusted debt ratio indicates a slightly better
debt position than does the unadjusted ratio.  The adjusted
ratio is a better indication of the debt position because of
the more realistic inventory and liabilities.


Chapter 11 - Problem 5 - Approximate Income If Inventory Had Been
                Valued At Approximate Current Cost

(a)   2001 Net income as reported                          $80,000,000

      Net increase in inventory reserve:
        2001 inventory reserve          $38,000,000
        2000 inventory reserve           32,000,000
(b)                                                         $ 6,000,000

(c)   Effective federal tax rate: $\frac{\$36,000,000}{\$116,000,000}$ = 31.0%

(d)   Change in taxes (b x c)                              $ 1,860,000

(e)   Net change in income (b - d)                        $ 4,140,000

(f)   2001 approximate income if inventory
      had been valued at approximate
      current cost (a + e)                                $84,140,000

Chapter 11 - Problem 6 - Computation of Z Scores

a.    Z = .012 ($90,000/$620,000) + .014 ($30,000/$620,000)
          + .033 ($55,000/$620,000) + .006 ($100,000/$280,000)
          + .010 ($440,000/$620,000)

$$Z = .012 \; (14.52) = .17$$
$$+ \; .014 \; (4.84) = .07$$
$$+ \; .033 \; (8.87) = .29$$
$$+ \; .006 \; (35.71) = .21$$
$$+ \; .010 \; (70.97) = .71$$

$$Z = 1.45$$

b.  The Z score is 1.45.  In a study that covered the period 1970-1973, a Z score of 2.675 was established as a practical cutoff point.  Firms that scored below 2.675 are assumed to have similar characteristics of past failures.

Chapter 11 - Problem 7 - Computation of Z Score

$$X_1 = \frac{\text{Working Capital}}{\text{Total Assets}} = \frac{(\$30,000 - \$18,000) \times 100}{\$88,000} = 13.64$$

$$X_2 = \frac{\text{Retained Earnings}}{\text{Total Assets}} = \frac{\$42,000 \times 100}{\$88,000} = 47.73$$

$$X_3 = \frac{\text{E.B.I.T.}}{\text{Total Assets}} = \frac{\$22,000 \times 100}{\$88,000} = 25.00$$

$$X_4 = \frac{\text{Market Value of Equity}}{\text{Book Value of Total Debt}} = \frac{(\$30 \times 8,000) \times 100}{\$38,000}$$

$$\frac{\$240,000 \times 100}{\$38,000} = 631.58$$

$$X_5 = \frac{\text{Sales}}{\text{Total Assets}} = \frac{\$125,000 \times 100}{\$88,000} = 142.05$$

$$Z = .012X_1 + .014X_2 + .033X_3 + .006X_4 + .010X_5$$

$$Z = .012 \times 13.64 = 0.16$$
$$.014 \times 47.73 = 0.67$$
$$.033 \times 25.00 = 0.83$$
$$.006 \times 631.58 = 3.79$$
$$.010 \times 142.05 = 1.42$$

$$Z = 6.87$$

# Chapter 12: Special Industries: Banks, Utilities, Oil and Gas, Transportation, Insurance, Real Estate Companies

Chapter 12 - Problem 1 - Supply the Words Necessary to Complete the Following Items

1. For a bank, nonperforming assets are assets for which the bank is not receiving _____ or is receiving _____ _____.

2. For a bank, reviewing the disclosure of the market value versus the book value of investments may indicate that investments have a market value substantially _____or _____ the book value.

3. For electric utilities, the balance sheet account Construction _____ ___ _____ is particularly important to the understanding of the utility statements.

4. For electric utilities, the income statement accounts Allowance for _____ _____ Used During Construction and Allowance for _____ _____ Used During Construction are accounts that relate to construction work in progress.

5. Oil and gas companies' financial statements are affected significantly by the method that they choose to account for costs associated with exploration and production. The method that they choose will be a variation of _____-_____ or _____-_____ methods.

6. The successful-efforts methods places only exploration and production costs of _____ wells on the _____ _____ under property, plant, and equipment.

7. With the full-costing method, exploration and production costs of ____ wells are placed on the _____ _____ under property, plant, and equipment.

8. The balance sheet format for air carriers, railroads, and motor carriers is _____ to that for a manufacturing or retailing firm.

9. For transportation firms, the income statement is a prescribed, categorized form of _____-_____ income statement.

10. Statutory accounting for insurance companies has emphasized the _____ _____ in its concern for protecting the policy holders by focusing on the _____ _____ of the insurance corporation.

11. Under GAAP the balance sheet of an insurance company is ____ classified by current assets and _____ _____.

12. The manner of recognizing revenue on insurance contracts is unique for the insurance industry. In general, the _____ of the _____ governs the revenue recognition.

13. Real estate companies contend that conventional accounting, recognizing _____ but not the underlying _____ of the property, misleads investors.

14. Some real estate companies have attempted to reflect _____ by disclosing _____ _____ in addition to the conventional accounting.


Chapter 12 - Problem 2 - Multiple Choice

Choose the best answer for each of the following questions and enter the identifying letter in the space provided.

_____ 1. All but one of the following would be a representative asset of a bank:

    a. investment securities
    b. loans
    c. equipment
    d. cash on hand
    e. savings accounts

_____ 2. All but one of the following would be considered an earning asset of a bank for the earning assets to total assets ratio.

   a. loans
   b. leases
   c. cash
   d. investment securities
   e. money market assets

_____ 3. This ratio for a bank provides an indication of management's ability to control the spread between interest income and interest expense:

   a. loan loss coverage ratio
   b. earning assets to total assets
   c. return on earning assets
   d. interest margin to average total assets
   e. equity capital to total assets

_____ 4. A ratio that indicates how funds are supplied to a utility is:

   a. return on assets
   b. percent earned on operating property
   c. operating ratio
   d. funded debt to operating property
   e. operating revenue to operating property

_____ 5. A ratio that relates net earnings to the assets primarily intended to generate earnings for a utility is:

   a. return on assets
   b. percent earned on operating property
   c. operating ratio
   d. funded debt to operating property
   e. operating revenue to operating property

_____ 6. For a utility, this ratio is basically an operating assets turnover ratio:

   a. return on assets
   b. percent earned on operating property
   c. operating ratio
   d. funded debt to operating property
   e. operating revenue to operating property

_____ 7. For a transportation firm, this ratio gives a measure of the source of funds with which property is obtained:

   a. operating ratio
   b. operating revenue to operating property
   c. long-term debt to operating property
   d. per mile-per person-per ton
   e. return on equity

_____ 8. Which of these industries have a uniform system of accounts?

   a. banks
   b. utilities
   c. transportation
   d. oil and gas
   e. a, b, and c

_____ 9. All but one of the following would be a representative liability of a bank:

   a. savings
   b. demand deposits
   c. cash on hand
   d. long-term debt
   e. time deposits

_____ 10. Typically, the largest expense for a bank will be:

   a. employer benefits.
   b. occupancy expense.
   c. salaries.
   d. provision for loan losses.
   e. interest expense.

_____ 11. This ratio indicates the extent of equity ownership in a bank:

   a. interest margin to average total assets
   b. loss coverage ratio
   c. loans to deposits
   d. equity capital to total assets
   e. deposits times capital

_____ 12. A ratio that indicates a measure of operating efficiency for a utility:

   a. operating revenue to operating property
   b. funded debt to operating property
   c. operating ratio
   d. percent earned on operating property
   e. long-term debt to operating property

_____ 13. This ratio is a measure of turnover of operating assets for a transportation firm:

   a. operating ratio
   b. long-term debt to operating property
   c. per mile-per person-per ton
   d. return on investment
   e. operating revenue to operating property

_____ 14. Insurance companies tend to have a stock market price at a discount to the average market price (price/earnings ratio). Which of the following is a likely reason for this relatively low market value?

   a. Insurance is a highly regulated industry.
   b. The insurance industry has substantial competition.
   c. The accounting environment likely contributes to the relatively low market price for insurance company stocks.
   d. The nature of the industry leads to standards that provide for much judgement and possible manipulation of reported profit.
   e. All of the above.

_____ 15. Which of the following have a balance sheet similar in format to a manufacturing firm?

   a. banks
   b. insurance companies
   c. utilities
   d. a and b
   e. none of the above

## Chapter 12 - Problem 3 - True/False

Indicate whether each of the following is true (T) or false (F) in the space provided.

_____ 1. A bank holding company may own bank-related financial services and nonfinancial subsidiaries.

_____ 2. Checking accounts or demand deposits are liabilities to a bank, since it owes the customers money.

_____ 3. Security transactions can have a major influence on the net income of a bank.

_____ 4. A bank can use security transactions to improve the loan loss coverage ratio.

_____ 5. Loan charge-offs increase the loan loss coverage ratio for a bank.

_____ 6. A low equity capital to total assets ratio for a bank indicates that the stockholders have a small investment in the bank in relation to the total assets of the bank.

_____ 7. The high deposits times capital ratio for a typical bank will indicate that the bank has a lot of debt in relation to its stockholders' equity.

_____ 8. A low loans to deposits ratio indicates that the bank is taking high risk.

_____ 9. Receivables collection is usually not a problem for utilities.

_____ 10. An increasing operating ratio is a positive indication for a utility.

_____ 11. An increase in the funded debt to operating property for a utility indicates an increase in the risk of the debt position.

_____ 12. Most of the traditional ratios also apply in the transportation field.

_____ 13. For a transportation firm, a rising operating ratio would be considered to be a positive trend.

_____ 14. A rising operating revenue to operating property ratio would be considered to be a positive trend for a transportation firm.

_____ 15. The passenger load factor can be an important profitability measure for an airline, due to the fixed cost nature of airline operations.

_____ 16. For an oil company, the full-cost approach would be considered to be a more conservative approach than the successful efforts approach.

_____ 17. Much subjectivity would need to be applied in reserve recognition accounting for an oil firm.

_____ 18. Insurance companies provide two types of service. One service is an identified contract service - mortality protection or loss protection. The second service consists of an investment management service.

_____ 19. Regulation of insurance companies started at the state level.

_____ 20. Statutory accounting has emphasized the income statement in its concern for protecting the policy holders by focusing on the financial solvency of the insurance corporation.

_____ 21. Statutory accounting practices developed much sooner for insurance companies than generally accepted accounting principles for insurance companies.

_____ 22. Real estate companies contend that conventional accounting, recognizing depreciation misleads investors.

_____ 23. Deferred policy acquisition costs represent the cost of obtaining policies. Under statutory accounting practices, these costs are deferred.

_____ 24. Insurance companies have been accused of over-reserving during very good years.

_____ 25. The manner of recognizing revenue on insurance contracts is unique for the insurance industry.


Chapter 12 - Problem 4 - Review of Bank

The following statistics are presented for 2002 and 2001 for Capital Bank:

| (in thousands) | 2002 | 2001 |
|---|---|---|
| Average net loans | $ 640,000 | $ 680,000 |
| Average total assets | 1,800,000 | 1,700,000 |
| Average earning assets | 1,200,000 | 1,100,000 |
| Average deposits | 960,000 | 990,000 |
| Average stockholders' equity | 76,000 | 72,000 |
| Interest expense | 82,000 | 80,000 |
| Interest income | 110,000 | 110,000 |

**Required:** a. For each year, calculate:
    1. deposits times capital
    2. loans to deposits
    3. equity capital to total assets
    4. interest margin to average earning assets
  b. Comment on the results in a, using the perspective of a shareholder.

Chapter 12 - Problem 5 - Electric Utility

Statistics from Toledo Electric Company annual report are presented below:

|  | (in millions) | |
| --- | --- | --- |
|  | 2002 | 2001 |
| Operating revenues | $285 | $270 |
| Operating expenses (including federal income taxes) | 220 | 205 |
| Federal income taxes | 18 | 15 |
| Interest deductions | 48 | 45 |
| Net income | 40 | 36 |
| Earnings available for common stock | 12 | 10 |
| Net plant | 800 | 720 |
| Current assets | 90 | 80 |
| Total assets | 900 | 860 |
| Shareholders' equity | 310 | 290 |
| Long-term debt | 360 | 310 |
| Current liabilities | 225 | 190 |
| Total liabilities and shareholders' equity | 900 | 860 |

**Required:**  a.  Compute the following ratios for 2002 and 2001:
1.  Funded Debt to Operating Property
2.  Times Interest Earned
3.  Operating Revenue to Operating Property
4.  Operating Ratio

b.  Comment on the above ratios for the two years.

# Chapter 12 - Problem 6 - Transportation Company

Gray Bus Company had the following operating results in the past two years:

|                           |    2002    |    2001    |
|---------------------------|-----------:|-----------:|
| Operating revenues        | $ 567,000  | $ 220,000  |
| Operating expenses        |   535,000  |   200,000  |
| Operating property        |   230,000  |   205,000  |
| Net income                |    20,000  |    15,000  |
| Long-term debt            |   230,000  |   195,000  |
| Estimated passenger miles | 3,000,000  | 2,600,000  |
| Load factor               |      61%   |      52%   |

**Required:**  a. For each year, calculate:
- 1. Operating ratio
- 2. Long-term debt to operating property
- 3. Operating revenue to operating property
- 4. Operating revenue to passenger-mile

b. Comment on the ratios in part (a).

c. Comment on the load factor.

Chapter 12 - Problem 7 - Successful Efforts vs. Full Cost

Little Oil Company made several drills for oil in 1999.  The following data represent its results:

|                    |              |
|--------------------|--------------|
| Total costs        | $24,000,000  |
| Total wells drilled| 20           |
| Good wells         | 14           |
| Dry wells          | 6            |

Assume that each well cost the same amount to drill.

**Required:**  a.  Determine the amount to be capitalized and the amount to be expensed if the successful-efforts method is used.

              b.  Determine the amount to be capitalized and the amount to be expensed if the full-cost method is used?

              c.  For the amount capitalized, when will it be expensed.

## CHAPTER 12 - SOLUTIONS

Chapter 12 - Problem 1 - Supply the Words Necessary to Complete
                        the Following Items

1.   income; reduced income

2.   above; below

3.   Work in Process

4.   Equity Funds; Borrowed Funds

5.   successful-efforts; full-costing

6.   successful; balance sheet

7.   all; balance sheet

8.   similar

9.   single-step

10.  balance sheet; financial solvency

11.  not; current liabilities

12.  duration; contract

13.  depreciation; value

14.  value; current value


Chapter 12 - Problem 2 - Multiple Choice

  e    1.   Savings accounts would be a representative liability of a
            bank.

  c    2.   Cash is not an earning asset of a bank for the earning
            assets to total assets ratio.

  d    3.   Interest margin to average total assets provides an
            indication of management's ability to control the spread
            between interest income and interest expense.

  d    4.   The ratio funded debt to operating property indicates how
            funds are supplied to a utility.

  b     5.    The ratio percent earned on operating property relates net earnings to the assets primarily intended to generate earnings for a utility.

  e     6.    For a utility, the operating revenue to operating property ratio is basically an operating assets turnover ratio.

  c     7.    For a transportation firm, long-term debt to operating property is a measure of the source of funds with which property is obtained.

  e     8.    Banks, utilities, and transportation firms have a uniform system of accounts.

  c     9.    Cash on hand would not be a representative liability of a bank.

  e   10.    Typically, the largest expense for a bank will be interest expense.

  d   11.    Equity capital to total assets indicates the extent of equity ownership in a bank.

  c   12.    The operating ratio indicates a measure of operating efficiency for a utility.

  e   13.    The operating revenue to operating property ratio is a measure of turnover of operating assets for a transportation firm.

  e   14.    All of the above are likely to be a reason for a relatively low market value for an insurance company.

  e   15.    None of the above types of companies have a balance sheet similar in format to a manufacturing firm.

## Chapter 12 - Problem 3 - True/False

| | | | | | | | | | |
|---|---|---|---|---|---|---|---|---|---|
| T | 1. | T | 6. | T | 11. | F | 16. | T | 21. |
| T | 2. | T | 7. | T | 12. | T | 17. | T | 22. |
| T | 3. | F | 8. | F | 13. | T | 18. | F | 23. |
| F | 4. | T | 9. | T | 14. | T | 19. | T | 24. |
| F | 5. | F | 10. | T | 15. | F | 20. | T | 25. |

Chapter 12 - Problem 4 - Review of Bank

a.1. Deposits Times Capital = $\dfrac{\text{Average Deposits}}{\text{Average Stockholders' Equity}}$

2002

$$\frac{\$960,000}{\$76,000} = 12.63\,\text{Times}$$

2001

$$\frac{\$990,000}{\$72,000} = 13.75\,\text{Times}$$

2. Loans to Deposits = $\dfrac{\text{Average Net Loans}}{\text{Average Deposits}}$

2002

$$\frac{\$640,000}{\$960,000} = 66.67\%$$

2001

$$\frac{\$680,000}{\$990,000} = 68.69$$

3. Equity Capital To Total Assets = $\dfrac{\text{Average Equity}}{\text{Average Total Assets}}$

2002

$$\frac{\$76,000}{\$1,800,000} = 4.22\%$$

2001

$$\frac{\$72,000}{\$1,700,000} = 4.24\%$$

4. $\dfrac{\text{Interest Margin To}}{\text{Average Earning Assets}}$ = $\dfrac{\text{Interest Margin}}{\text{Average Earning Assets}}$

2002

$$\frac{\$110,000 - \$82,000}{\$1,200,000} = 2.33\%$$

2001

$$\frac{\$110,000 - \$80,000}{\$1,100,000} = 2.73\%$$

b.   Deposits to capital has fallen, providing a safer position for shareholders (favorable). Loans to deposits decreased slightly (unfavorable). Equity capital to total assets decreased slightly (unfavorable). Interest margin to average earning assets decreased (unfavorable).

Chapter 12 - Problem 5 - Electric Utility

a.

1.   Funded Debt To Operating Property = $\dfrac{\text{Funded Debt (Long - Term)}}{\text{Operating Property}}$

   2002

   $\dfrac{\$360}{\$800} = 45\%$

   2001

   $\dfrac{\$310}{\$720} = 43.06$

2.   Times Interest Earned = $\dfrac{\begin{array}{c}\text{Recurring Earnings, Excluding}\\ \text{Interest Expense, Tax Expense,}\\ \text{Equity Earnings, and Minority Earnings}\end{array}}{\begin{array}{c}\text{Interest Expense, Including}\\ \text{Capitalized Interest}\end{array}}$

|  |  | 2002 | 2001 |
|---|---|---|---|
| Operating revenues |  | $285 | $270 |
| Operating expenses (including federal income taxes) |  | 220 | 205 |
| Federal income taxes |  | ( 18) | ( 15) |
| Operating expenses before taxes |  | 202 | 190 |
| Operating income | (A) | 83 | 80 |
| Interest deduction | (B) | 48 | 45 |
| Times interest earned | (A)/(B) | 1.73 Times | 1.78 Times |

3.   Operating Revenue to Operating Property = $\dfrac{\text{Operating Expenses}}{\text{Operating Revenue}}$

   2002

   $\dfrac{\$285}{\$800} = 35.63\%$

   2001

   $\dfrac{\$270}{\$720} = 37.50\%$

4.   Operating Ratio = $\dfrac{\text{Operating Expenses}}{\text{Operating Revenue}}$

   2002

   $\dfrac{\$220}{\$285} = 77.19\%$

   2001

   $\dfrac{\$205}{\$270} = 75.93\%$

b.   Funded Debt to Operating Property increased, indicating a less favorable debt position. The interest coverage declined, indicating a lesser ability to cover the debt. The firm is generating slightly less revenue on its operating property. Operating expenses have increased in relation to revenue.  The ratios indicate a worsening of the financial position.

## Chapter 12 - Problem 6 - Transportation Company

a.

|  |  | 2002 | 2001 |
|---|---|---|---|
| 1. Operating Ratio = | $\dfrac{\text{Operating Expenses}}{\text{Operating Revenue}}$ | $\dfrac{\$535,000}{\$567,000}$ | $\dfrac{\$200,000}{\$220,000}$ |
|  |  | 94.36% | 90.91% |
| 2. Long - Term Debt To Operating Property = | $\dfrac{\text{Long - Term Debt}}{\text{Operating Property}}$ | $\dfrac{\$230,000}{\$230,000}$ | $\dfrac{\$195,000}{\$205,000}$ |
|  |  | 100.00% | 95.12% |
| 3. Operating Revenue To Operating Property = | $\dfrac{\text{Operating Revenue}}{\text{Operating Property}}$ | $\dfrac{\$567,000}{\$230,000}$ | $\dfrac{\$220,000}{\$205,000}$ |
|  |  | 2.47 Times | 1.07 Times |
| 4. Operating Revenue To Passenger - Mile = | $\dfrac{\text{Operating Revenue}}{\text{Passenger - Miles}}$ | $\dfrac{\$567,000}{3,000,000}$ | $\dfrac{\$220,000}{2,600,000}$ |
|  |  | 18.90¢ | 8.46¢ |

b.   The operating ratio has risen, showing a decline in profitability.  The percentage of debt has increased in relation to operating property.  Revenue to property shows a higher turnover; hence, this company's problem is not in generating sales, but rather in cost control.  Revenue per passenger-mile has risen, showing price increases.

c.   The load factor indicates that the buses were more full in 2002 than in 2001.

## Chapter 12 - Problem 7 - Successful Efforts vs. Full Cost

a.   $\dfrac{14 \text{ Good Wells}}{20 \text{ total Wells Drilled}} = 70\%$

70% x $24,000,000 = $16,800,000 - capitalized amount

30% x $24,000,000 = $7,200,000 - expensed amount

b.   Capitalize all $24,000,000

c.   The amount capitalized will be expensed in subsequent periods as oil is removed.

# Chapter 13: Personal Financial Statements and Accounting For Governments and Not-for-Profit Organizations

Chapter 13 - Problem 1 - Supply the Words Necessary to Complete the Following Items

1. For personal financial statements, _____ _____ information is considered to be more relevant than _____ _____.

2. The basic statement prepared for personal financial statements is a _____ ___ _____ _____.

3. For the statement of financial condition, assets are presented at estimated _____ _____, and liabilities are stated at estimated _____ _____.

4. For personal financial statements, the statement of changes in ____ _____ presents the major sources of increases and decreases in ____ _____.

5. The accounting for nonprofit institutions is ____ uniform from one type of institution to another, and sometimes it is ____ even uniform within a particular type of _____.

6. The accounting for a profit-oriented business is centered on the _____ concept and the efficiency of the _____. The accounting for a nonprofit institution does ____ include a single _____ concept or _____.

7. Government transactions are recorded in one or more funds designed to emphasize _____ and _____ limitations.

8. When reviewing the financial reporting of governmental units, it is helpful to visualize the reporting in a _____ _____.

9. Nonprofit institutions other than governments use forms of financial reporting that _____ from the _____ _____ of system to a _____ _____ of reporting.

10. Some nonprofit institutions have added budgeting by objectives and/or measures of _____ to their financial reporting to incorporate measures of _____.

# Chapter 13 - Problem 2 - Multiple Choice

Choose the best answer for each of the following questions and enter the identifying letter in the space provided.

_____ 1. Which of the following is an example of a profit institution?

     a. bank
     b. state government
     c. church
     d. university
     e. none of the above

_____ 2. Proprietary funds are a type of funds used by governments. A reasonable definition of proprietary funds is as follows:

     a. funds that are intended for maintaining the assets through cost reimbursement by users, or partial cost recovery from users and periodic infusion of additional assets
     b. funds whose principal must remain intact
     c. funds that handle all cash receipts and disbursements not required to be accounted for in another fund
     d. funds that cash receipts and disbursements related to the payment of interest and principal on long-term debt
     e. none of the above

_____ 3. Government transactions are recorded in one or more funds designed to emphasize control and budgetary limitations. A fund may be established for which of the following specific purpose:

     a. highway maintenance
     b. parks
     c. debt repayment
     d. endowment fund
     e. all of the above

_____ 4. Which of the following, in accounting for governments, provides necessary resources and the authority for their disbursements?

     a. encumbrances
     b. restricted funds
     c. proprietary funds
     d. special assessments
     e. appropriations

_____ 5. For a statement of changes in net worth, which of the following would be a realized increase in net worth?

    a. dividend income
    b. change in value of land
    c. decrease in value of house
    d. personal expenditures
    e. none of the above

_____ 6. For a statement of changes in net worth, which of the following would be an unrealized increase in net worth?

    a. increase in value of land
    b. decrease in value of furnishings
    c. personal expenditures
    d. salary
    e. none of the above

_____ 7. Which of the following is **not** a suggestion for reviewing the statement of financial condition?

    a. Review realized decreases in net worth.
    b. Review the net worth amount.
    c. Determine the amount of the assets that you consider to be very liquid.
    d. Observes the due period of the liabilities.
    e. Compare specific assets with any related liabilities.

_____ 8. Which of the following is **not** a suggestion for reviewing the statement of changes in net worth?

    a. Observe the due period of the liabilities.
    b. Review realized increases in net worth.
    c. Review realized decreases in net worth.
    d. Observe whether the net realized amount increased or decreased and the amount.
    e. Review unrealized decreases in net worth.

_____ 9. Which of the following would be a source of information for personal financial statements?

    a. bank statements
    b. checkbooks
    c. real estate tax returns
    d. insurance policies
    e. all of the above

_____ 10. Which of the following would **not** be an acceptable presentation on a personal financial statement?

        a. A car may be presented at cost.
        b. Payables and other liabilities are presented at the discounted amounts of cash to be paid.
        c. Investments in real estate should be presented at their estimated current values.
        d. The liability for income taxes payable should include unpaid income taxes for completed tax years and on estimated amount for income taxes accrued for the elapsed portion of the current tax year to the date of the financial statements.
        e. All of the above.

## Chapter 13 - Problem 3 - True/False

Indicate whether each of the following is true (T) or false (F) in the space provided.

_____ 1. Personal financial statements are financial statements of individuals, husband and wife, or a larger family group.

_____ 2. Statement of Position 82-1 concludes that the primary users of personal financial statements normally consider estimated current value information to be more relevant for their decisions than historical cost information.

_____ 3. SOP 82-1 concludes that personal financial statements should present assets at their estimated current values and liabilities at their estimated current amounts at the date of the financial statements.

_____ 4. The statement of financial condition is similar to the income statement.

_____ 5. On a statement of financial condition, the assets are presented at historical cost.

_____ 6. For the statement of financial condition, the assets are presented at historical cost, and liabilities are stated at estimated current amounts.

_____ 7. On the statement of financial condition the difference between the total assets and total liabilities is designated net worth.

_____ 8. For personal financial statements, the statement of changes in net worth is required.

_____ 9. The statement of changes in net worth is presented in terms of realized increases (decreases) and unrealized increases (decreases).

_____ 10. Personal financial statements include a statement of personal income.

_____ 11. On a statement of financial condition, the figure that will be most important is the net worth amount.

_____ 12. The accounting for a nonprofit institution is centered on the entity concept and the efficiency of the institution.

_____ 13. The accounting for a profit-oriented business and a nonprofit institution have a bottom line - net income.

_____ 14. In accounting for governments, encumbrances are future commitments for expenditure.

_____ 15. In accounting for governments, fiduciary funds are funds whose principal must remain intact.

_____ 16. Government transactions are recorded in one or more funds designed to emphasize control and budgetary limitations.

_____ 17. Governments must do their accounting using a modified accrual basis.

_____ 18. For governments, the budget is merely a plan of future revenues and expenses.

_____ 19. For governmental units, bonds backed by the full faith and credit of the governmental unit are industrial revenue bonds.

_____ 20. Nonprofit institutions other than governments use forms of financial reporting that vary from the fund type of system to a commercial type of reporting.

_____ 21. Accounting for nonprofit institutions does not typically include the concept of efficiency.

_____ 22. Budgeting by objectives and/or measures of productivity could be added to the financial reporting of nonprofit institutions.

            Definitions                               Terms

_____ 1.   The principal of these              a. Appropriations
            funds must remain intact.
            Typically revenues earned
            may be distributed.

_____ 2.   All cash receipts and               b. Debt service
            disbursements not required
            to be accounted for in another
            fund.

_____ 3.   Operations that are similar         c. Capital projects
            to private businesses where
            service users are charged fees.

_____ 4.   Cash receipts and disbursements     d. Special
            assessments
            related to the acquisition of
            long-lived assets.

_____ 5.   Provide necessary resources         e. Internal services
            and the authority for their
            disbursements.

_____ 6.   Future commitments for              f. Enterprises
            expenditure.

_____ 7.   Intention is to maintain            g. Proprietary funds
            the fund's assets through
            cost reimbursement by users,
            or partial cost recovery from
            users and periodic infusion
            of additional assets.

_____ 8.   Service centers that supply         h. General fund
            goods or services to other
            governmental units on a
            cost reimbursement basis.

_____ 9.   Cash receipts and disbursements     i. Fiduciary funds
            related to improvements or
            services for which special
            property assessments have
            been levied.

_____ 10.  Cash receipts and disbursements     j. Encumbrances
            related to the payment of
            interest and principal on
            long-term debt.

# Chapter 13 - Problem 5 - Statement of Financial Condition

For Linda and Bob, the assets and liabilities and the effective income tax rates are as follows at December 31, 2002:

| Account | Tax Bases | Estimated Current Value | Excess of Estimated Current Values Over Tax Bases | Effective Income Tax Rates |
|---|---|---|---|---|
| Cash | $30,000 | $30,000 | -- | -- |
| Marketable securities | 40,000 | 50,000 | 10,000 | 30% |
| Residence | 130,000 | 150,000 | 20,000 | 20% |
| Royalties | -0- | 10,000 | 10,000 | 20% |
| Furnishings | 40,000 | 30,000 | (10,000) | -- |
| Auto | 20,000 | 15,000 | ( 5,000) | -- |
| Mortgage payable | 60,000 | 60,000 | -- | -- |
| Auto loan | 4,000 | 4,000 | -- | -- |

**Required:** a. Compute the estimated tax liability on the differences between the estimated current value of the assets and liabilities and their tax bases.

b. Present a statement of financial condition for Linda and Bob at December 31, 2002.

# Chapter 13 - Problem 6 - Statement of Changes in Net Worth

For Jackie and Joe, the changes in net worth for the year ended December 31, 2002, are detailed as follows:

| | |
|---|---:|
| Realized increases in net worth: | |
|   Salary | $40,000 |
|   Dividend income | 1,000 |
| | |
| Realized decreases in net worth: | |
|   Income taxes | 6,000 |
|   Personal expenditures | 30,000 |
| | |
| Unrealized increases in net worth: | |
|   Marketable securities | 6,000 |
|   Residence | 8,000 |
| | |
| Unrealized decreases in net worth: | |
|   Furnishings | 5,000 |
|   Car | 4,000 |
|   Estimated income taxes on the differences between the estimated current values of assets and the estimated current amounts of liabilities and their tax bases | 8,000 |
| | |
| Net worth at the beginning of year | 50,000 |

**Required:** Prepare a statement of changes in net worth for the year ended December 31, 2002.

# CHAPTER 13 - SOLUTIONS

## Chapter 13 - Problem 1 - Supply the Words Necessary to Complete the Following Items

1. current value; historical cost

2. statement of financial condition

3. current values; current amounts

4. net worth; net worth

5. not; not; institution

6. entity; entity; not; entity; efficiency

7. control; budgetary

8. pyramid fashion

9. vary; fund type; commercial type

10. productivity; efficiency

## Chapter 13 - Problem 2 - Multiple Choice

___a___  1. A bank is an example of a profit institution.

___a___  2. A reasonable definition of a proprietary fund is a fund that is intended for maintaining the assets through cost reimbursement by users, or partial cost recovery from assets and periodic infusion of additional assets.

___e___  3. Funds established for a specific purpose would include highway maintenance, parks, debt repayment, and endowment.

___e___  4. In accounting for governments, appropriations provides necessary resources and the authority for their disbursements.

___a___  5. For a statement of changes in net worth, dividend income would be a realized increase in net worth.

___a___  6. For a statement of changes in net worth, an increase in the value of land would be an unrealized increase in net worth.

___a___  7.  Reviewing realized decreases in net worth is not a
              suggestion for reviewing the statement of financial
              condition.

___a___  8.  Observing the due period of the liabilities is not a
              reasonable suggestion for reviewing the statement of
              changes in net worth.

___e___  9.  Bank statements, checkbooks, real estate tax returns,
              and insurance policies would be a source of
              information for personal financial statements.

___a___ 10.  Presenting a car at cost would not be an acceptable
              presentation on a personal financial statement.

Chapter 13 - Problem 3 - True/False

| T | 1. | T | 7.  | F | 13. | F | 19. |
|---|----|---|-----|---|-----|---|-----|
| T | 2. | F | 8.  | T | 14. | T | 20. |
| T | 3. | T | 9.  | T | 15. | T | 21. |
| F | 4. | F | 10. | T | 16. | T | 22. |
| F | 5. | T | 11. | F | 17. |   |     |
| F | 6. | F | 12. | F | 18. |   |     |

Chapter 13 - Problem 4 - Accounting for Governments - Match
              the Terms to the Definitions

| i | 1. | j | 6.  |
|---|----|---|-----|
| h | 2. | g | 7.  |
| f | 3. | e | 8.  |
| c | 4. | d | 9.  |
| a | 5. | b | 10. |

Chapter 13 - Problem 5 - Statement of Financial Condition

a.    Marketable securities      $10,000 x 30% = $3,000
      Residence                  $20,000 x 20% =  4,000
      Royalties                  $10,000 x 20% =  2,000
                                                           $9,000

b.

Linda and Bob
Statement of Financial Condition
December 31, 2002

| | |
|---|---:|
| Assets: | |
| Cash | $ 30,000 |
| Marketable securities | 50,000 |
| Residence | 150,000 |
| Royalties | 10,000 |
| Furnishings | 30,000 |
| Auto | 15,000 |
| Total assets | $285,000 |
| | |
| Liabilities: | |
| Mortgage payable | $ 60,000 |
| Auto loan | 4,000 |
| Total liabilities | 64,000 |
| | |
| Estimated income taxes on differences between estimated current value of assets and their tax basis | 9,000 |
| | |
| Net worth | 212,000 |
| Total liabilities and net worth | $285,000 |

Jackie and Joe
Statement of Changes in Net Worth
For the Year Ended December 31, 2002

Realized increases in net worth:
 Salary              $40,000
 Dividend income          1,000
                  41,000

Realized decreases in net worth:
 Income taxes           6,000
 Personal expenditures       30,000
                  36,000

Net realized increases in net worth    5,000

Unrealized increases in net worth
 Marketable securities       6,000
 Residence            8,000
                  14,000

Unrealized decreases in net worth
 Furnishings           5,000
 Car              4,000

Estimated income taxes on the
 differences between the estimated
 current amounts of liabilities and
 their tax basis          8,000
                  17,000

Net unrealized decreases in net worth   3,000
Net increase in net worth        2,000
Net worth at the beginning of the year   50,000
Net worth at the end of the year     $52,000